Praise of Nature Speaks

"Each of the elegant poems in *Nature Speaks* provide a thoughtful pathway through the dense forest of cultural and ecological challenges we face as a species. Deborah Kennedy shows us how to artistically navigate our way with her beauty-making of words and images as we strive to live in harmony with Nature in these most critical of times. Stunning!"
  —Osprey Orielle Lake, sculptor, founder and president of Women's Earth and Climate Caucus, author of *Uprisings for the Earth: Reconnecting Culture with Nature*

"*Nature Speaks* offers us the vast and infinite world, our history, our earth, both gorgeous and dying. To read Deborah Kennedy's *Nature Speaks* is like waking up from a dream to find that someone around us is wide awake. "What hole is deep enough to throw away the whole world?" the author asks in a searing poem, followed by a rich, echoing drawing. The art following each poem has a science illustrator's detail and a visionary artist's dream. In this work we find Enlightenment women, hawk moths, ancient goddesses, acorns, millions of prairie bison, melting sea ice, watersheds, pollinators, mass extinctions, plastics, breast milk, the solar system, egrets, turtle eggs, ancient footprints, tule grass, redwoods. *Nature Speaks* looks at the whole beautiful world, and refuses to look away from its suffering. 'Dare to think', we are reminded, and after reading this book, we do."
  —Carolyn Brigit Flynn, author of *Communion: Poems in Praise of the Sacred Earth*

Nature Speaks

Art & Poetry for the Earth

Nature Speaks

Deborah Kennedy

Live green!
Deborah

WHITE CLOUD PRESS
ASHLAND, OREGON

White Cloud Press titles may be purchased for educational, business,
or sales promotional use. For information, please write:

White Cloud Press
PO Box 3400
Ashland, OR 97520
www.whitecloudpress.com

Cover and interior design by Christy Collins, C Book Services
Copyright © Holocoenotic Image, Dr. W. D. Billings, used with permission.

First printing: 2016
16 17 18 19 20   10 9 8 7 6 5 4 3 2 1

Printed in South Korea

Library of Congress Cataloging-in-Publication Data

Names: Kennedy, Deborah, 1953- author.
Title: Nature speaks : art & poetry for the earth / Deborah Kennedy.
Description: Ashland : White Cloud Press, 2016.
Identifiers: LCCN 2016027135 | ISBN 9781940468464 (paperback)
Subjects: LCSH: Nature--Poetry. | BISAC: NATURE / Ecology.
Classification: LCC PS3611.E5577 A6 2016 | DDC 811/.6--dc23
LC record available at https://lccn.loc.gov/2016027135

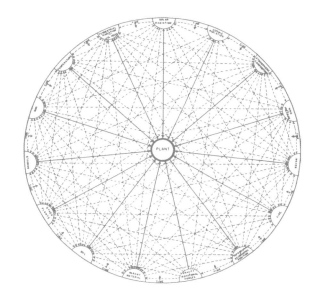

Dedicated to my family, large and small.

With thanks to my Mother for telling me
she always wanted me to be a writer.

Holocoenotic Circle of Environmental Complexity, Dr. W. D. Billings

Contents

Acknowledgements

Flowing down from the Sierra, the fast-moving white water of the Yuba River charges through granite boulders, shaping the landscape and nurturing life. For me, the Yuba is a metaphor for the powerful stream of ideas that have helped form and sustain my thinking, and have guided me toward a fuller understanding of our often chaotic world. Here are some of the authors who have been strong currents in my Yuba River and have my enduring gratitude:

Barbara Tuchman's *The March of Folly* helps me feel more patient with our current ecological folly as she skewers the history of human foibles with unerring aim and a touch of humor.

Rachel Carson's life and work teaches me about courage and honesty, the power of one voice and the complexities of our uneasy relationship with chemicals.

Rianne Eiseler's *The Chalice and the Blade*, reveals the conflicting narratives that inform our culture and gives me hope we may return to being a more cooperative society based on partnership rather than dominator models.

Fritjof Capra's *The Web of Life* illuminated the natural world's self-organizing web of life and how our own lives are tightly entwined with the intricate and complex processes of natural systems. His work helped lay the conceptual foundation for many of my projects.

Gary Snyder's mix of art and poetry and bold calls for environmental action inspire me. He is a rugged trail guide using the arts to point out what we have lost and where we need to go to rediscover a healthier relationship with the larger natural world.

Gary Paul Nabhan's *Cultures of Habitat: On Nature, Culture and Story*, is rooted in the often hidden history of the indigenous people of the West and their relationship with the land. His lively and warm writing transforms my daily experience, thinking and work.

I am especially grateful to my family: To my mother and father, Joanne and Starrett Kennedy, whose call, "Let's take a walk," fostered a love for the birds, woods, fields and lakes. They gave me the freedom to explore the open spaces and to follow my creative impulses; to my brother and sisters for their encouragement. Also, to my own family, the foundation of my life — my husband, Dale Larson, a great spirit, with positive energy, a keen editorial eye, and unflagging support for my creative visions, and our son, Evan Kennedy Larson, an invaluable source of wry humor, perceptive critiques, personal warmth and integrity.

Special thanks to my friends: Julia Claus, for her vision and sturdy station wagon that brought me West to my life on the edge; Katherine Levin-Lau, for her nurturing joie d'vivre and thoughtful artistic reflection through the years; Lynne Stromberg for her bright spirit, wise counsel, and listening to all my stories, even the very long ones; and Eve Page-Mathias, for supporting my artistic projects and my teaching at San Jose City College.

The California Arts Council, The Arts Council of Silicon Valley, Sybase and the Compton Fund have generously assisted my creative career. My artist residencies with Walter Bischoff Galerie, New Pacific Studios and WORKS have offered important periods of reflection and growth. Christine and Dennis Richards, leaders of the Willow Glen Poetry Project and the lively and talented poets in the group continue to provide a crucible to share and refine my work. Parthenia M. Hicks has been a thoughtful guide, and sensitive editor throughout. Kathleen McClung, author of *Almost the Rowboat* and recipient of numerous poetry awards including the Rita Dove Poetry Award, insightfully contextualized the book and gave me the gift of a thoughtful and deeply perceptive reading. Rose Offner worked with great enthusiam as a book design and publishing consultant, and is an invaluable source of vision and advice.

Also, I am deeply appreciative of Steve Scholl and all the folks at White Cloud Press for believing in my work and using their remarkable talents to launch *Nature Speaks* into the larger currents of ideas, art, and poetry that are, hopefully, carrying us closer to a more caring relationship to our home, the Earth.

Foreword
by Kathleen McClung

Honoring moon and sun and all that grows on earth, *Nature Speaks: Art and Poetry for the Earth* offers us the opportunity to savor Deborah Kennedy's artistry and urgency in not one but two branches of creativity — visual art and lyrical poetry. Kennedy is widely known in California and beyond for solo and group shows of her paintings, sculptures, mixed media, and large-scale installations. Her first public artwork, titled *Ecotech* commissioned in the early 1990s for a new public transit line in Silicon Valley, consisted of a six-ton boulder cut into thick slabs, embodying a key concept of holistic thinking, the relationship between the parts and the whole. She etched and inlaid mesmerizing images into the surface of the huge, polished stone and topped one slab with bronze casting, emphasizing the relationship of technology and nature.

Since that influential public art project — still installed in the city of San Jose — she has continued focusing both her art and her poems on the most pressing ecological themes of our time — climate change, species extinction, cancers from toxic chemicals, as well as our interconnectedness and pathways to healing. I love the arc and architecture of this book, which moves from praising the fundamental web of life in Part One to mourning a damaged and "sinking world" in Part Two to decrying the poisons surrounding and within our bodies in Part Three to encouraging vital new thought and action in Part Four.

The journey we take through this extraordinary book is challenging but ultimately rewarding and revitalizing, as all life-changing journeys are. We see horrors — "wings fold / like crumpled paper, birds plummet from the skies" and "Breast milk is now / tainted, hidden poisons / in a mother's gift." And yet we also see images of hope — "Hummingbirds defend beads of nectar crowning my Mexican sage" and "white violets/ dance like tiny angels / on the point of a pin." Kennedy serves as a passionate, perceptive guide on a journey across time, a journey encompassing floodwaters in Brazil, Colombia, Pakistan, Thailand, Romania, edges of machetes that catch sunlight in the Congo, a jet droning on its way to Australia, Darwin's "proper London air," and the forests, trails, and gardens close to our homes.

As a reader, I admire not only the expansive scope of *Nature Speaks*, but also the balance Kennedy strikes between reason and mystery: we hear in her book a deep respect for the findings and warnings of science and a reverence for metaphor and symbol. The alluring pen and ink images that she couples with each poem vary in concept and style from realistic to surreal, embodying beautifully this balance between the known and the unknown, the proven and the possible. A very different artist/poet in an earlier, less perilous age, William Blake, shared a similar genius on the page.

Kennedy's poems have been likened to those of Gary Snyder, Kenneth Rexroth, and Robinson Jeffers — all Californians attuned to the gifts and scars of the earth. I hear echoes, too, of Adrienne Rich in Kennedy's poems, particularly "Chalice" and "DNA Rules" and "Fate of my Son" that explore the complex weave of mothering, living, feeling, and thinking in a rapidly changing world. Both Rich and Kennedy give precise words to that which seems just past our reach. Both creative women inspire us as individuals and communities to fuller contemplation and bolder action in addressing local and global environmental problems.

The provocative, sumptuous poetry and art of *Nature Speaks* awaken us to "hear the coyote's chorus under the aspen's stir" and to sense in our bodies how "each thicket pulses with the beat of nature's deep redemption." Listen. Turn the page. Discover ancient kin and the newborn. Then listen some more.

Introduction

This book reflects my ongoing artistic journey that has taken me from working with large-scale installations and paintings to expressing myself with the writing and illustrations of this book. My early installations and objects drew on social and political themes, including human rights and censorship. In 1989, just before the Berlin Wall fell, I created a series of installations on its surface. These installations included *Writing on the Wall*, in which I gathered hopes and fears from people in West Berlin, East Berlin, and the United States, inscribed these statements on metal plaques, and mounted them on the Wall. *Writing on the Wall* allowed the inner thoughts and feelings of people from both sides of Berlin and from both sides of the Atlantic to communicate together on the Wall. This work garnered considerable attention and was featured in newspapers and books.

In the early1990s I created *Ecotech*, a public artwork for a new transit line in San Jose, California. In my research for this project, I became fascinated with efforts to reform our technological systems and manufacturing so they function in biocompatible ways. With *Ecotech*, I had found a way to express my abiding concern for the natural world through my artwork. Since then, my work has primarily explored environmental subjects. My conceptually-based work begins with questions: What new ways of thinking can help us solve our environmental problems? How is exposure to toxic chemicals affecting the health of human and animal populations? How are birds, butterflies, and amphibians faring in our increasingly technological world with its burgeoning human populations? Researching these questions is the way I discover the ideas, images, and materials that inform and inspire my work.

In 1999, I created a show entitled *Nature Speaks* for the de Saisset Museum. The exhibit featured three large-scale installations and the work was very demanding. While also teaching, and raising a young child, I did most of the considerable labor myself. People appreciated the show, and the work seemed to have an impact on my community. *Artweek*, a regional art magazine, published a review and an interview with me about this work. Overall, however, the impact did not seem commensurate with the effort.

This exhibition spurred me to evaluate my role as an artist. I wanted to express myself in a new way that would speak more directly about my ideas and feelings. The condition of the natural world and the threats to human health are at a critical juncture today. To express myself in the most powerful way I could, I began to write poems. This choice may seem paradoxical, but I believe poetry has a secret power.

As a society we often seem largely unmoved by our environmental challenges despite many rational arguments. Poetry speaks through metaphors which can move our hearts, and then our brains. Therefore, I began writing about these themes, and my experiences with the natural world, and found this work deeply satisfying.

After several years of working on these poems, I decided to create a pen and ink illustration for each one, a new discipline for me. Some of these illustrations required up to 40 or more hours of work. I found the long process of gradually building up gradations in value and defining the forms both meditative and enjoyable. My drawings frequently illustrated a metaphor or an image in the poem, and I approached each one anew, creating images that vary from realistic to surreal. I used earth-toned inks like burnt sienna, originally made of specially colored soils and sepia inks to create these drawings and am enamored of their deep, warm browns. Sepia ink, originally made from the ink of cuttlefish, often appears in the first European landscape drawings.

After completing several illustrations, I began to experiment with wet-into-wet techniques, where ink seeps and spreads in water on the surface of the paper. I also started to use spattering, where little drops of ink are sprayed at the image, often requiring detailed masks. These techniques recall the Dadaists' and Surrealists' experimentation with "chance operations," such as squishing paint between two surfaces to develop patterns with little artistic control. The Surrealists felt these techniques allowed the randomness of the real world to enter into their artwork. Their use of "chance operations" often affronted traditionalists who emphasized using the skillful artistic techniques found in academic European art. For me, these techniques suggest today's increasingly unpredictable world and the uncontrolled movement of unseen materials throughout the environment.

My experience as an artist has affected my writing beyond creating the illustrations. I have worked on these poems for many years, shaping and honing them countless times. This reminds me of the many stages of alabaster stone carving. I start with a hammer and a steel tool called a point to rough out the shape, and next move to stone chisels and claws to start refining the form, followed by files and coarse rifflers, which look like small, shaped files. These rifflers help refine the final shapes. Polishing requires six grades of sandpaper, each worked methodically over the entire surface. This sculptural process informs my writing-working and reworking the poems, seeking the essential story, the right tone, image, and word.

By publishing this work, I hope to help confront our troubled relationship with the natural world and support the growing edge, where we, as a global community, can create new visions that will help solve our environmental problems. By changing our beliefs and behaviors as individuals and communities, we can restore and regenerate our planet.

Living Inside the Circle
Every Part Wedded to the Whole

"When we try to pick out anything by itself, we find it hitched to everything else in the Universe."

JOHN MUIR

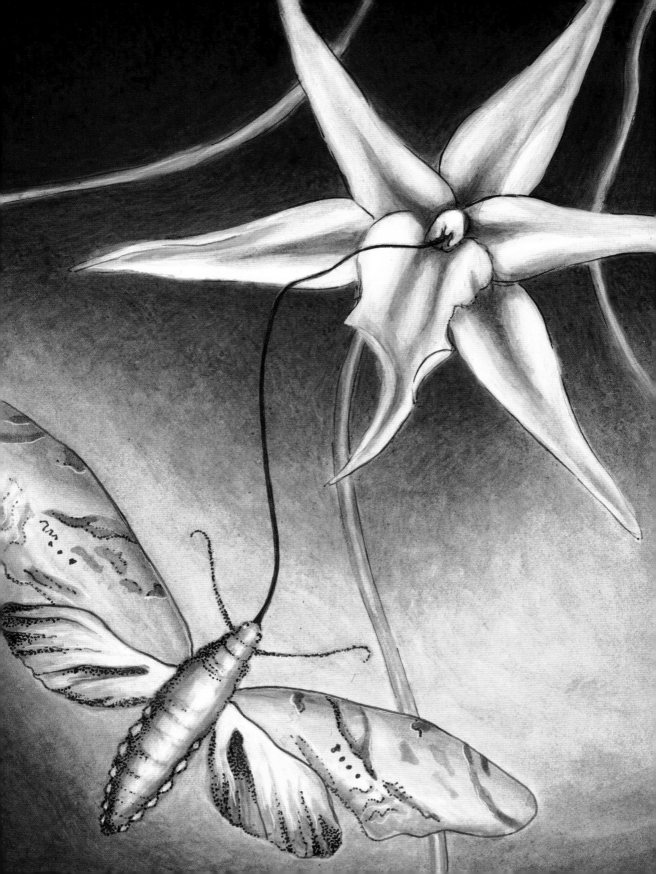

Coevolution

Darwin walked beneath iron arches and crystal sky,
the dangerous, liquid scent of distant jungles

hanging heavy in the proper London air.
In Kew Gardens, the conservatory, a cathedral grand

dedicated to botany, he gazed upon the Star of Bethlehem,
an orchid, exiled from the heights of Madagascar.

Each petal carved from ivory's gleam, blooming
in the velvet night. Beneath the celestial petals grow

strange spurs, nectaries, green whips hanging
twelve inches long, tips wet with juice, the honeyed lure.

From the negative, Darwin saw the positive.
He wrote, "Good Heavens, what insect could suck it?"

Only an insect with a proboscis, a nose improbable,
one-foot long. His revelation met with waves

of ridicule crashing from Britain to the Continent.
Laughter rippled through forty years until the night

an entomologist with animal eyes, silently waiting
high in the trembling jungle, captured the shadow

of the hawk moth. Its shaggy wings, eight inches wide,
beat through layered leaves following the scent of musk.

The hawk moth hovered before the radiant Star,
its slender snout coiled tight, unfurled its length,

probed down the orchid's spur, sipped the nectar,
and bore away a fine coat of pollen. Darwin's vision,

a spark through golden amber, orchid and moth in eager
embrace, two bound as one, across eons' arc.

About Coevolution

Charles Darwin, naturalist and author of *The Origin of Species*, encountered an orchid with an unusual feature — foot-long hollow tubes hanging beneath the blossoms, the tips filled with nectar. Darwin realized that the pollinator for this flower must have an equally long snout, or proboscis, to be able to reach the nectar and fertilize the flower. Darwin was ridiculed for this preposterous idea — imagine the sight of a poor insect attempting to fly while sporting a foot-long proboscis — until just such a moth was discovered. The Hawk Moth flies with its snout coiled in a tight ball, and unfurls this dexterous appendage to delicately probe the orchid's hanging nectaries. In part, through his encounter with this orchid, he began to formulate the theory that species can form long-term evolutionary relationships leading to extraordinary and mutually beneficial transformations and unique dependencies. All life has slowly and patiently evolved over the eons, exquisitely adapting to a challenging world. How will we continue to successfully evolve in a world we are so rapidly transforming?

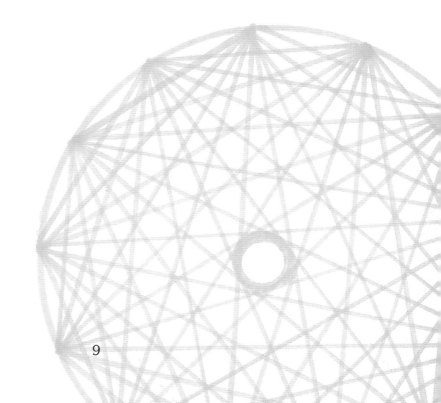

Web of Life

Dedicated to Dr. W. D. Billing, originator of the
Holocoenotic Theory of Environmental Complexity

Bind together the blooming air, water dancing
from pole to frozen pole. The sun's touch
brings light to steamy life. The loamy earth,

the patient plants and all the animals, secret
family wed by blood. The sacred fire lights
the dark and leaves pure ash. Spin each thread,

strong and supple, every strand lit with honey's glow,
weave the cloth, an endless circle. Here and there,
you and me, all the ones who came before,

ancient kin to every pilgrim who walks the path.
Life, long and loud, sings and whistles, croaks and
howls. In our metal days, machine and man

clash and grind. This once fine cloth, used so hard,
gaping holes torn side to side. Edges fray
like fine down feathers. Our broken fingernails,

black with grease, knuckles grazed with scars,
bind each living fiber, mend the tears, renew the web,
until the deserts hum with life and leaf again.

About
Web of Life

Dr. W. D. Billings, a professor of Life Sciences, researched botanical environments and illustrated his holistic theory with an intricate line drawing. He modeled the complex, interdependent relationships that foster life and showed how all parts of the web of life are deeply entwined and work together to create functioning ecosystems. Ecosystems consist of interdependent communities of living plants and creatures with their supportive physical environments. All life on our planet, including humans, is sustained through complex relationships with our ecosystems. We are dependent on the natural world for our survival, and our personal actions and inactions affect our planet's health, and then in turn, our own. This poem's illustration includes part of Dr. Billings's circular scientific illustration, and several key forces making all life possible — the sun, pollen, water, and the atmosphere.

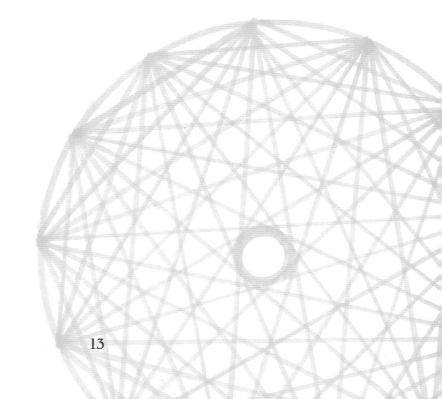

Double Vision

I.
Raising crystal eyes to a vestal sky, endless web
of silver lake blue, untouched by time, but rent by rock
stone arches surge to broken crests, etched and scarred.

Wandering tangled streets, chilled water from ancient aqueducts
sits like a polished river rock in my belly. Rome, past and present,
picked over bones of an endless feast. Entering the sunken

stone orb, home to all the gods, the sweeping span leads eyes up
to a shaft of light piercing a pounding oculus. The sun coils
at my still feet, slowly burning an elipse into the stone floor.

II.
Twenty years pass, my feet flat on my own land, the full moon
rises to a blazing zenith, hovers at the center of the sky
dressed in sheer clouds, circled by a halo, ice and crystal light.

The nine circles of heaven spin, etched against a raven sky
my tender hand, shadow on this sterling disk, feels every echo
beat against the stone, bearing swelling life, full and aching.

Each open eye, each yielding nerve, reaches, straining
to see, to hear, the land lying beyond this thin veil
all around the breath of an unheard, whispering world.

About
Double Vision

This poem juxtaposes two experiences separated by twenty years and six thousand miles. The first was visiting the Pantheon, one of the best preserved ancient Roman temples. The interior of this remarkable concrete building is an almost perfect sphere one hundred and forty-three-feet-high and wide. The curving walls lead up to an oculus, or twenty-seven-foot-wide circular opening, at the top of the dome. Oculus means "eye" in Latin, and this opening acts almost like an eye's pupil, creating an opening to the sky and bringing dramatic shafts of light into the interior. The second experience was seeing a full moon ringed by a glowing ice halo. These halos form when cirrus clouds spread thin layers of ice crystals high up in the atmosphere where they reflect the moonlight. Enthralling visions like moon-bows and ice halos often hover above us, but they are less frequently seen in a world dazzled by millions of moving screens. The drawing is an interior view of the Pantheon, light streaming through its oculus.

Sign Language

Every word made clear by her darting
hands, wiry fingers fan out, palms turn up

pausing for a beat, then with a little flutter,
as if to say, "Really, what can you expect?"

Curling, rolling, tracing splines, pulling meaning
from lucid air. Her fingers arch, slowly curve back

like the liquid neck of a startled heron. Both hands
fly up, reaching higher. Suddenly silent, they drop

heavily to her thighs and quietly curl together,
two sleeping doves, still in the dusty, dim cote.

She leans forward listening, one hand leaps up
stabbing the air, her fingers taut, raptor stiff,

the sign language of bone and blood,
the cry of a hunting falcon's wing.

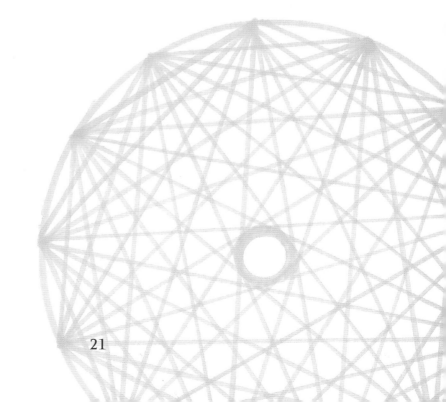

About
Sign Language

This poem was prompted by watching the eloquent hand gestures of a woman on a train in Australia. Her graceful curving motions reminded me of the movement of birds — actually not surprising because birds, bats, and humans have the same set of bones in our forearms. From humeri to phalanges, we all use the same working parts given us by common ancestors, but specialized to suit our own individual tasks. Recent research reveals other ways we are closely related to other life forms. In 2004, scientists discovered humans share approximately sixty percent of our genes with Red Jungle Fowl, the ancestral species of all domestic chickens, and even more astonishing, we share almost twenty-five percent of our genetic material with wine grapes. This research illustrates the deep fusion between humans, animals and plants — the result of our common inheritances from distant ancestors. This profound kinship we share with all life on our planet should inspire us to respect and foster all species.

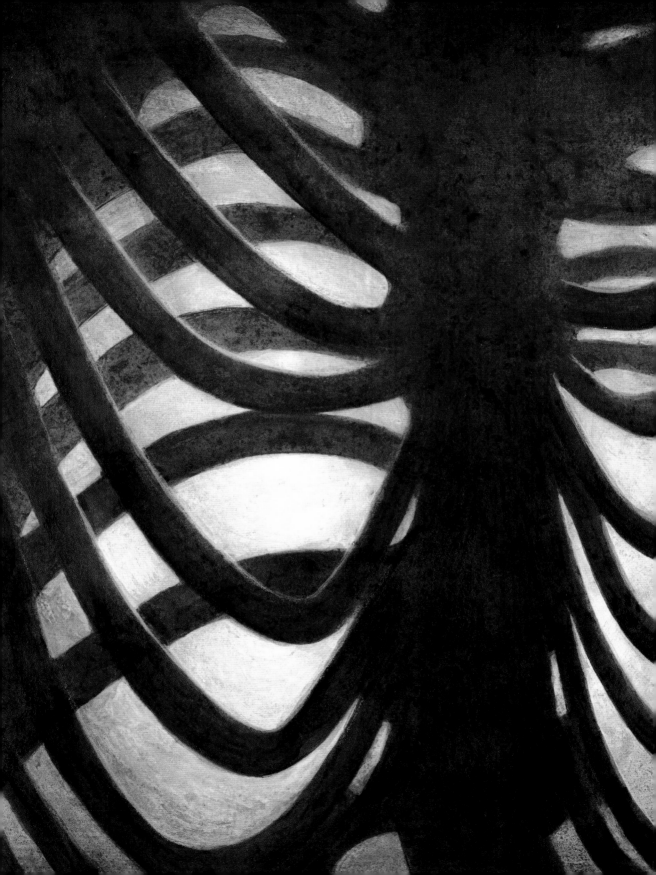

Bone Shadows

Translucent fingers, feathery trees reach out to me
trembling in the breeze, moving inside of my eyes
vibrating the clear glass fibers binding me together.

Breathing inside the pale, grey leaves, moving gently
alive in this moment, the scent of sesame seeds soaks inside
skin rich as an Egyptian queen. Suddenly, there is no space

between my warm flesh and the atom air caressing me.
Sunlight casts shadows of my bones. I eat no food
no red fruit or flesh, I eat my grief and give birth to new life.

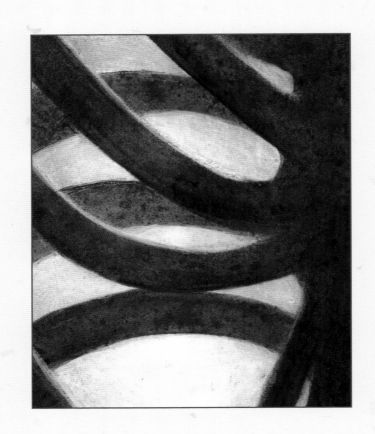

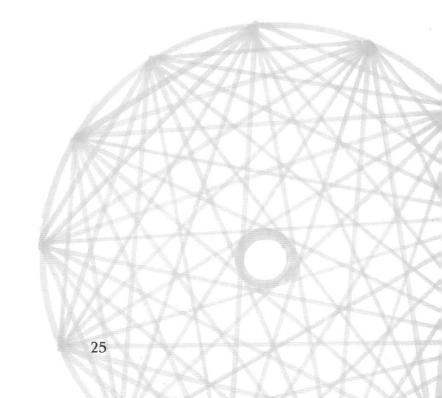

About
Bone Shadows

This poem describes the transcendent moment when the barriers between the self and the natural world evaporate. The last line refers to the complex myth of the ancient Aztec goddess, Tlazolteotl. Sculptures often show her crouching in the final stages of childbirth, grimacing, as her infant's head emerges. This compelling image is surely one of the only sculptures depicting this pivotal moment of childbirth. In some versions of her story, she eats the filth of the world, or its sins, and creates new life from these base elements. The story of this intriguing Aztec goddess encourages me to create new visions and art from our dark ecological realities. This myth connects me to the cycles of life, and the powerful forces of transformation and regeneration.

Rough-legged Hawk

Flash of white, taut wings dart
across the sky, coming to a dead stop.
Head a still point against the blue.
Not a Red-tail, Harrier, or Cooper.

The silhouette etched in my mind
blunt head, four-foot wingspan
flight feathers long as a hand.
Hovering, he beats his wings

like a man driving nails into solid oak.
The hawk turns, shifts uphill
with a kill light stare, hunts for
a flash of fur, a glint of an upcast eye.

Spins, drops, hovers again, the hawk
banks hard, wings pitch right
wheels away, disappears over the hill
tears the last air from my lungs.

About
Rough-legged Hawk

This "walking poem" records my encounter with an Arctic hawk on a hill above the valley where I live. Even for casual birders, like myself, seeing a new bird is exciting. The image of this hunting hawk remains emblazoned in my memory. I was riveted by the raptor's intense focus, its broad white wings pumping up and down, its head utterly still against the sky. Rough-legged hawks currently have stable population levels, unlike many other raptors or birds of prey. By protecting bird populations and their habitats, we will gift future generations with similar moments of revelation. This artwork features the silhouette of a rough-legged hawk's four-foot-wide wingspan. The many layers of spattering suggest the tiny, interconnected pieces of a vital ecosystem.

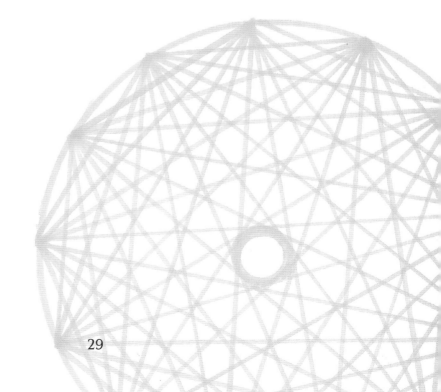

Sweet Water to Salt

Each drop wends its way
from the crest of the hill
down to this small pond
the edge of the end.
Water doing what water does.

Yellow musk blooms in the seep,
a pair of mallards, his feathers gleam
like teal satin, hers all modest browns
spin in stately circles,
courtiers dancing the minuet
nodding with careful courtesy.

The still water flows down
spills free over cliff's edge
rushes over the last brink,
wind gusts blow crystal beads
straight up to the sky.
They hang for half a breath
and then fall to ocean surge.

Every drop finds its way,
at last, sweet water wedded
to salt sea, turning, returning
following the sun's driving beat.

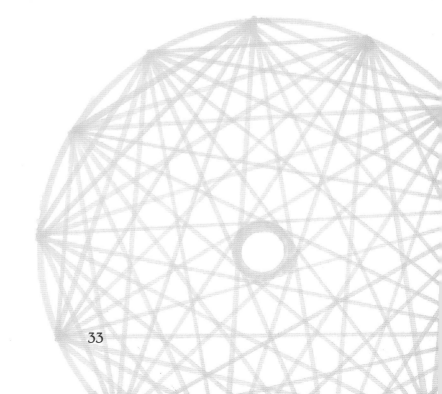

About
Sweet Water to Salt

Environmentalists know the health of watersheds is vital to the health of our communities and the natural world. A watershed is an area of land, usually a valley with surrounding hills, where surface water collects, then drains into a common outlet. The upper edge is the crest of the nearby mountains or hills. The lower edge is the ocean, bay, or river that receives the moving water. Watersheds provide innumerable natural benefits, including gradually moving sediment to lower areas, creating and enriching the soil. The lowlands of a watershed, called wetlands, help to filter and purify water, providing cleaner water for plants, animals and people. I went in search of the lower boundary of a local watershed where fresh or sweet water joins the sea and found several along the coast. The rendering records the end of a watershed with a cliff and a small waterfall joining the rolling waves of the Pacific Ocean.

Careless Hands
Wreaking and Reaping

*"But man is a part of nature, and his war against nature
is inevitably a war against himself."*

RACHEL CARSON

Teeming

Sailors crowd the starboard bow
pointing across the sea
paved with turtle shells
glinting like wet, black cobblestones.
Fish packed the rivers, mouths
gaping, fighting for breath in the scrum.
Teeming, steaming, dreaming.

A quilt of birds covered the bay.
Beating hearts take flight
a sky black with wings, the sun a ghost.
Feeding, breeding, seeding.
Men shot into the air, no need to aim
like heavy rain the bodies fell.
Racket, clack it, crack it.

Sixty million bison once thundered
across the open prairie
their massive heads
a fortress against wolf and bear
but not the .45-70 Government rifle.
In just a hundred years
only half still galloped across
their sea of grass.

In another hundred years
only two thousand buffalo still stood.
The trains rolled east
loaded high with stinking hides.
Men in bowler hats posed arms akimbo
on top of mounds piled thirty feet high
sixty wide, all bison skulls, horn and bone
white as shells scoured clean by sun.
Recruiting, shooting, looting.

In a place beyond time sliced by money
hear the bells ringing for an emerald hour
feel the blood rush through your living heart.
Grounding, resounding, abounding.

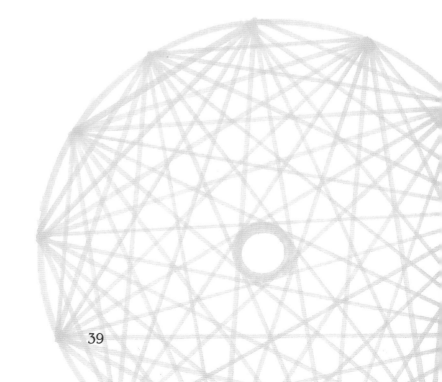

About
Teeming

Early claims of extraordinarily abundant wildlife in the Americas can seem like travelers' tall tales, yet multiple eyewitnesses confirm those claims. European explorers described entire bays covered with the glistening backs of sea turtles and streams roiling with fish. Unfortunately, these explorers rapidly hunted several species to extinction. This loss of wildlife, even entire species, continues today, yet there are glimmers of hope. The primary cause of habitat loss — the explosive growth rate of human populations — has slowed and may decline in upcoming decades. Another positive development are the efforts to restore and protect damaged habitats often fostering swift increases in populations of birds and other animals. With a commitment to habitat restoration and controlling our own populations, perhaps the wildlife in the Americas will again astound us. The artwork reflects on the poem's metaphor: San Francisco Bay covered by a quilt of birds.

Quorum Sensing

Ten thousand auks, black and white, Deco sharp,
rush across the rocks with penguin's waddle
and dive into the sea, tracing arcs beneath
the dark water, churning ice and foam.

Sinew strung taut, no eye can see the lines
spun of feather's down, leathery tendons knit
the flock into one. Clucking throughout the day,
We must eat, we must eat now.
We must go, we must go now.
Are you there? Yes, I am here.

Then the sailors came, hardened by years
of hauling cold, wet ropes. They pressed north
to stone islands in inky seas. Herded the awkward
auks to holding pens. Labored, year after year,
backs slick with sweat, twisted necks, plucked
their fingers raw, boots slipping on red rock.

Auk's soft cries through the day, through the night,
Are you there? I am here.
Are you there? I am here.
All here? All here?

No, shredded the sinews. No, snapped the tendons.
No, sapped the will of the wings, hammering
a hole in hearts that once beat as one.
Search through tangled thread, twisted, sheared
and shredded, stretching to the horizon.

Seek the three blind sisters, stay fate's hand,
lay down the blade, and spin a cord of fire
across this midnight sea, find that burning yes again.

About Quorum Sensing

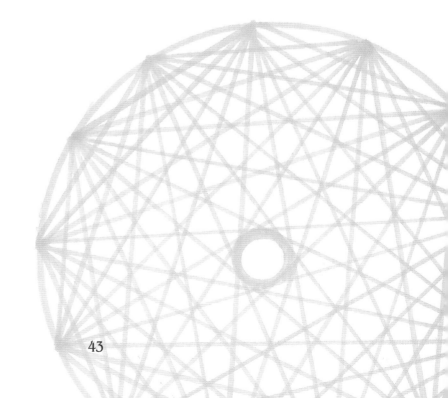

In the 1700s, Europeans piously believed it was not possible for humans to destroy a species created by God. However, in the 1800s, people hunted the great auks to extinction and proved humans are indeed capable of extinguishing an entire species. The great auks once lived in the Far North and had populations estimated to have been in the millions. They were large flightless birds, reminiscent of penguins but with long, slender necks. Auk lived on fish; ungainly on land, but swimming with powerful grace underwater. Biologists believe that once the flock's size fell to fewer than ten thousand birds, they lost the ability to make group decisions. This phenomenon, called quorum sensing, is defined as a system used by large, leaderless populations to make intelligent group decisions and coordinate behavior. This group process requires a minimum population level and should inform our current efforts to preserve other similar species. The drawing is a silhouette of a great auk filled with the metaphorical invisible threads that once knit this species into a thriving community.

Gilt Frames

In a tourist town
sleek color photos
set in golden frames
show creamy fur against
crisp white snow. A
polar bear posing with her twins
amuses idle urban explorers.

Today, the Arctic's daily ebb
is gone, blue ice gushes
with cutting water,
bitter salt seas drown
beneath glacial rivers.
No one recites epic poems
of the frozen past.
Only polar bears remember
a Spartan life of infinite cold
hunting seal and staining ice
with rich red blood.

The world is turning south
ice packs shear and crash.
Light on the water
where no water should be.
Light on the water
sears dark eyes
glints off teeth
bleached by hunger.
Heavy paws pull against
an endless swell, searching
for the vanquished ice.

We must drink
from this sullied course,
raise our goblets to the ruin.
Welcome Lethe's gentle gift
sit and watch the shadows
drift across this chrome sea.

About
Gilt Frames

Climate change is threatening the world's population of polar bears. Arctic polar bears are especially vulnerable. They live and hunt seals on ice packs — large spans of ocean covered by thick layers of floating ice. Global warming is melting the sea ice, and an area equal to the combined size of Alaska, Texas, and Washington has already disappeared. This loss of ice packs is one of many serious threats to polar bear populations. Sadly, today, many bears are in poor health due to the deteriorating conditions in their habitats. Polar bears are great swimmers, often crossing thirty-mile stretches, and reportedly at times swimming two hundred miles of sea. Yet now, polar bears and their cubs increasingly drown in the open water, unable to travel the even longer distances necessary to reach the remaining ice packs. The image contrasts the ornate golden frames surrounding gallery photographs of polar bears that inspired this poem with an empty Arctic Ocean, stripped of ice packs and polar bears.

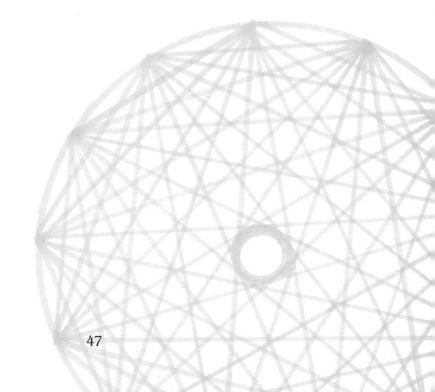

Midnight Garden

Walking through my midnight garden
I inhale the first scent of jasmine,
tender as a mother stroking the pulsing

crown of her newborn's head.
The second breath, sickly sweet
like soft candy stuck to my back teeth.

Turning, a sudden strike inside my gut,
this summer, so few Monarchs, so few
Swallowtails now careen over sunset poppies.

At the breakfast table, in the morning
I numbly read cool quotations,
one-third of butterflies gone in just ten years.

Memories fade in one generation.
Papillon, leptir, farfett, vlinder, kapu-kapu
hushed in every far-flung tongue.

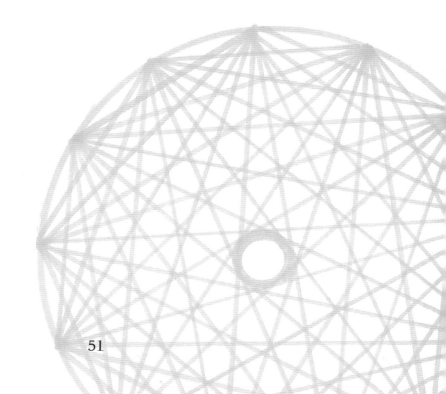

About
Midnight Garden

Rapid drops in butterfly populations and increasing species extinctions, are happening worldwide. Fewer and fewer butterflies are bringing their moments of delight to our yards and open fields. Butterflies and moths are important to a thriving ecosystem; they pollinate many native plants and human crops and are important food sources for birds and bats. Numerous projects and organizations are working to stabilize our butterfly populations. Citizens can support these efforts by creating backyards that welcome and feed beleaguered butterflies. The artwork features a monarch butterfly, once common in my area. At the bottom of the page wet-in-wet ink work suggests the remarkable process of a butterfly's metamorphosis.

Paper Wings

"The fate of animals is…indissolubly connected with the fate of men."
ÉMILE ZOLA

Yesterday, no one watched the river of red-winged blackbirds
flowing southward, the hawks' spinning on a rising wind

or the arc of an osprey's wing diving into open water. Tonight
the seven o'clock news tells the story of birds falling from the sky

around the globe. The TV screen briefly shows, in black of night,
lolling heads, dirty piles of wet feathers, fished from muddy water

by men in vinyl suits. Unpreened feathers hang strangely heavy.
All the result of natural causes, pliant faces repeat again and again

as they map contagion's spread, night by night. They will not
read the acid acronyms PCB, DDT, PBDE. They will not even

whisper the cool, round syllables of carbamate, selenium, or mercury.
They will not point to colored diagrams of chemical tracks etched

through bones and burnt through bodies' shields. Wings fold
like crumpled paper, birds plummet from the skies. Men, faces

covered with white masks, stuff bodies in plastic sacks stretched tight
and full, heave bags into the back of trucks, heavy tires spray loose gravel.

What hole is deep enough to throw away the whole world?
The quiet spreads in wetlands, woodlands, and flyways reaching

north and south. Like smoke in still autumn air, the question rises:
if the wind of birds is empty, how will the flesh of my flesh take flight?

About
Paper Wings

"Avian decline" is the scientific term for our loss of birds and bird species from the environmental disarray quietly sweeping the globe. Recent studies predict that by the end of our current century, one-quarter of all bird species will be extinct. The loss comes primarily from human activity. Construction and extraction industries destroy natural areas; food sources are contaminated by the use of pesticides and herbicides; and birds perish when they collide with power lines, windmills, and windows. The combined impact of these challenges is leading not only to precipitous declines in many bird populations, but also to profound hazards to ourselves. The image depicts a central metaphor of this poem — paper wings — suggesting the fragility of birds, and indeed, all life.

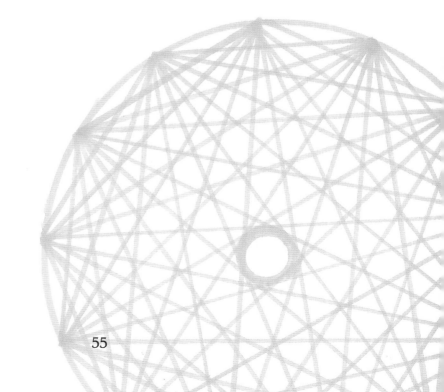

Vacation Apocalypse

Hammered into my seat on a thirteen-hour flight to Australia, the sticky traces of my guilt spray out into the troposphere behind the grinding plane. A woman in a head scarf embroidered with black-beaded flowers sits beside me. Beyond her daughter chatters, pink toes, curling, translucent petals in the overhead light.

The mother and I talk easily despite breathing air from two different worlds. We meander through our children and our travel plans. Then, I say, "Before coming to Australia, all I heard about was the killer heat wave in Sydney, the raging bush fires and cyclone floods too far South. I was starting to wonder, if I was going on

vacation in a climate change apocalypse!" She smiles faintly, and her eyes flicker toward her daughter's head, cradled in her lap, "Is anyone doing anything about it?" I look inside for a glimpse of hope, "Not really, not the scope and scale of change we need. Many people are trying, but recently a U. S. senator on the Congressional

science panel said we don't need to worry because God promised Noah there wouldn't be anymore floods. For me, this doesn't pass the test as a scientific policy point in the 21st century." She didn't reply, her head scarf suddenly looming between us and we both fell silent, only the drone of the plane's jet engines continued our conversation.

About
Vacation Apocalypse

This poem reflects on my thirteen-hour flight from California to Australia. Jet flight is a normal contemporary activity and many people are blissfully unaware of the serious pollution generated by jets. These planes have a greater negative impact on climate change than any other form of travel when estimated per passenger mile. A large proportion of a plane's greenhouse gases are emitted at a high altitude, where they have a powerful impact on the atmosphere and global warming. For someone living in an unsustainable society, yet striving to be more environmentally conscious, normally pleasant activities can engender a cascade of conflicted feelings. The visual interpretation shows the silhouette of a jet above the folds of a head-scarf, highlighting one more theme in the poem — the cultural divides that make consensus on environmental concerns difficult today.

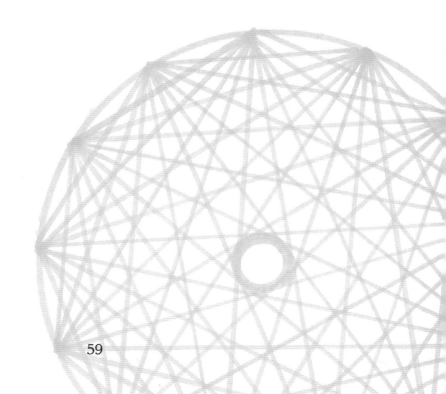

Hole Minus Hole

Each frozen word, like biting ice cubes until
my metal teeth stab down to the roots.
Colony collapse disorder, avian decline,

global warming — the heat of rage can not live
in these formal phrases. Each word a tool, ripping meaning
from a sinking world, stripping my syntax of all feeling.

Crisis, decline — quiet lies. Really a plan, a strategy,
a fat bankroll, more like dinner for seven billion people.
Admit it, don't you secretly find those last lusty birds

singing at dawn annoying anyhow? Like a newly
pulled tooth, my tongue probes, checking and
rechecking the pulpy hole, feeling for what is not there.

About
Hole Minus Hole

Why aren't more people seriously concerned about our ecological challenges despite the many media reports on our mounting environmental problems? Perhaps part of the trouble is our media and scientists, trying to be extremely objective, strip all emotion from their reporting. A recent VICE news segment called "Greenland is Melting" brought this into sharp relief for me. At one point the interviewer and a researcher stood on an immense field of rapidly melting ice discussing the increasing rate of the melting and ensuing sea-level rise. Then the scientist said, very softly, "Sometimes I feel so frightened when I see all of this." I thought, "This is what is missing. We attach so little emotion and sense of urgency to the way we talk about these issues." We can gravely underestimate the extent of our problems if we are primarily concerned that scientists might be overly alarmist or exaggerating their claims. The swirling image here is the top of a massive hurricane, one of the many severe weather events we will see more of in a world threatened by escalating climate change.

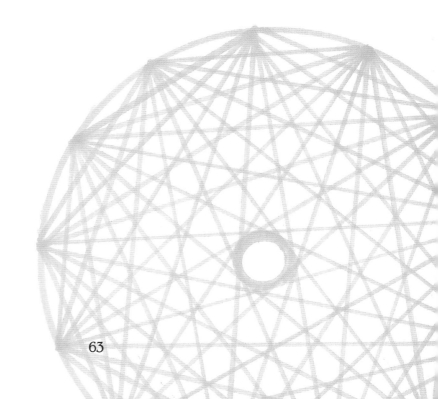

La Femme Savant

Sunlight through yellow leaves, the early heat promises a scorching day.
This morning should be cool muffled gray, sitting at my computer,
sinking into a swill of pixels, reading brief histories of enlightened women
and the deluge of news, trawling for the most despicable morsels
to share at dinner. Words ricochet inside my electronic echo chamber,
each plain thought sinks in a torrent of static. Science scorned as "just a theory,"
deceptions swirl like muddy water across a billion screens.

Where is the glittering hostess of the Republic of Letters,
Enlightenment savant reborn in heliotrope brocade edged with Flemish lace,
head balanced on an ivory neck? With wry riposte, she reviles
this willful descent of modern medieval minds spewing mouthfuls
of cold gruel and old lard in every headline. With wicked retort
cut through their clamor. Remember the world is not a digital dream,
nature equals food, times seven billion mouths.

My fingers click, my eyes twitch as the electronic news pulse tells all,
floodwaters churn in Brazil, Colombia, Pakistan, Thailand, Romania
and in China that coal-burning miracle too. Wisconsin farmlands
planted and harvested by broad worn hands for six generations
turn to rushing turbid toxic rivers. All followed by dust-bowl droughts
around the world. Texans burn in parched fields and call for more ardent prayer.

Talking heads dismiss all research round the globe, confusing lonely facts for a body of
knowledge. My phantasm philosopher proposes, "If you wish to live outside
the fierce embrace of the Enlightenment, if you ridicule the cautious computations
of weathercasters from the four directions, then renounce all the merciful gifts of science.
No four hours of heart surgery or dainty dentistry. Do not even sip from our
endless electronic fountains or gaze at our shimmering screens.
Sit silent in your dark dank cells praying to absent gods while we heal the sky."

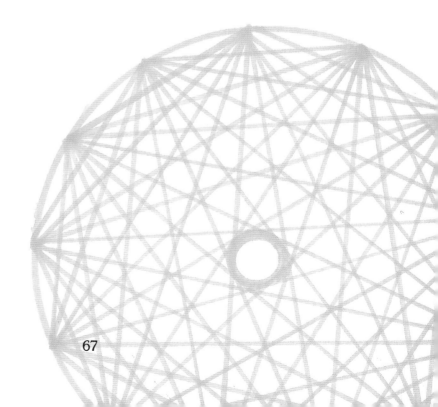

About
La Femme Savant

In the 18th century France was the one of the main centers of a dynamic cultural and political movement, the Enlightenment. This movement laid the conceptual groundwork for the American Revolution and still influences liberal thought today. The proponents of the Enlightenment championed the rights of individuals and believed dialogue, education, and open access to information was the path toward social progress. The leading thinkers of this movement congregated in coffee shops — the new public meeting places that percolated with rebellious ideas and rang with the cry, "Dare to think." Femmes savants, the learned women of the day, also created salons where intellectuals could meet and sharpen their ideas in challenging, yet civil, meetings. A few of these women became significant authors and helped shape the thinking of the day. Here I envision a resurrected femme savant who contests today's climate change deniers. The rendering features this learned woman and in the distance a vignette from a recent photograph of a flash flood with a mother and her son clinging to the roof of a car in rapidly rising waters.

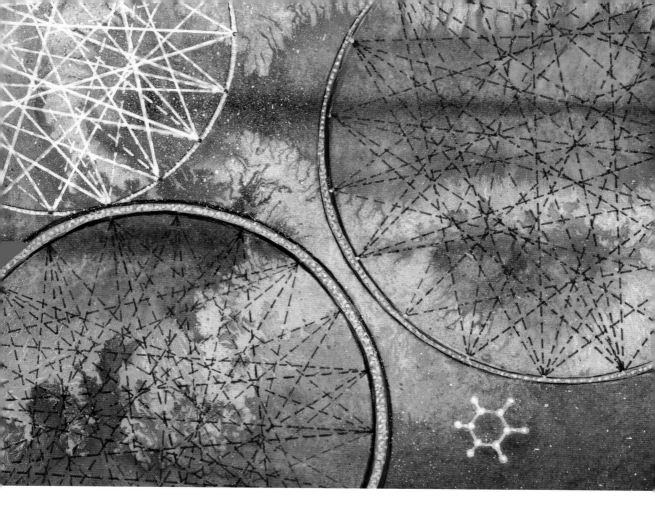

Beautiful Poisons
Bearing the Burden

"Imagine if, for the last 50 years, we had sprayed the whole earth with a nerve gas. Would you be upset? Would I be upset? Yes! I think people would be screaming in the streets. Well…we've done that. We've released endocrine disruptors throughout the world that are having fundamental effects on the immune system, on the reproductive system. We have good data that show that wildlife and humans are being affected. Should we be upset? Yes – I think we should be fundamentally upset. I think we should be screaming in the streets!"

DR. LOUIS J. GUILLETTE, JR.

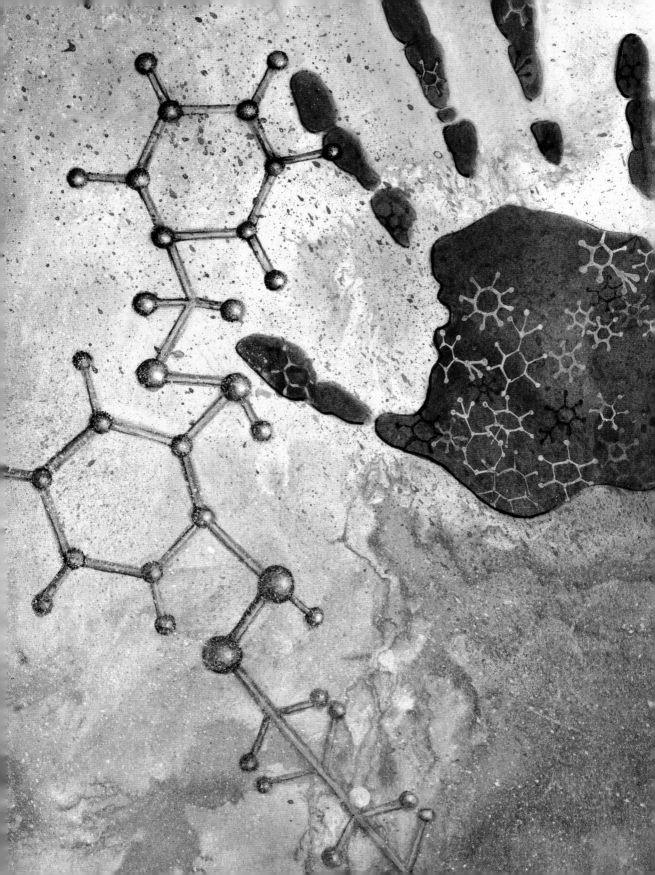

Secrets

My secrets, your secrets, all our secrets,
like warm, brittle eggs, rotten inside.
Crack them open, the stench arises.
Every tribe, every nation hides the seeds
of its own ruin in these fragile vaults.

Now, only scientists can read the ciphers,
tell the story of our rubbery umbilical
cords pumping crimson juice,
spinning the fibers of a growing body,
building the lost labyrinths of a brain.

Only the makers and breakers
keep the hidden lists, patiently testing
our first blood, tainted by a wizard's brew
from factory and lab. Unseen atoms spin,
shards of swallowed glass in ruby vessels.

Phalates in shampoo, in sweet perfume,
in your new car, benzene, toluene, leaving
sticky fingerprints on all we touch.
A million molecules, beyond our sight,
crack the helix, shred the pattern.

A vinyl curtain hanging in the shower,
the soft white pillow for your head,
plastic food on every plastic table.
A million molecules, beyond our sight,
crack the helix, shred the pattern.

Couples huddle in empty houses,
listening for cries that never come.
Mothers long for all the days
they will not see, as a traitor
slowly grows within. Little girls

with strangely budding breasts,
autistic boys turning, turning
wide eyes upon a world unseen.
We hide the seeds in fragile vaults,
my secrets, your secrets, all our secrets.

About
Secrets

Today, our air, water, and soil, as well as many consumer products, expose us to toxic materials. All humans, even people living far from cities and industrial areas, carry the residue or "body burden" of potentially harmful substances in their bodies. Studies find the blood, fats and other body fluids of adults, children, and even newborns have hundreds of detectable chemical residues, many well-known for toxic effects. The health impact of exposure to these materials can include infertility, thyroid disease, cancer, asthma, psychological disorders, as well as birth defects and learning disabilities in offspring. Chemical exposures also contribute to the rising incidence of obesity, heart disease, and diabetes.

On June 22, 2016, President Obama signed the Frank R. Lautenberg Chemical Safety for the 21st Century Act, a law that replaced a disastrously inadequate law crafted in 1976. At long last, this new law requires chemical companies to review the safety of the chemicals used in commerce and requires special protections for pregnant women and children, populations especially vulnerable to serious negative health effects from unregulated chemicals. Also, the law affords the Environmental Protection Agency new and more effective tools to regulate the safety of the estimated tens of thousands chemicals currently imported, used, or manufactured in the United States. However, only informed, persistent, and widespread action by citizens will guarantee the firm enforcement of these regulations and begin to reduce the toxic burden affecting future generations. The illustration portrays a "sticky handprint" with ball and stick models of common chemicals.

Return of Bona Dea

Please, do not fear, I must be quite a sight stepping out of the darkness into your warm circle. Your fire dancing in the dark forest, your faces flickering in the light reminded me of olden times, I came to visit. So much has changed, I know, few of you remember me, it has been ages. When I see you gathered round the fire, I remember waking in the hot night,

my chest sweaty, sheets bound around my restless legs, rising eager for the midsummer celebrations — festivals of the sun — the sun, gift to all life. When the heat of the summer finally baked the chill of winter out of our bones, this was a reason to celebrate. When we tasted the first ripe fruits, the sweet juice you had not sucked for a year, this was reason to celebrate.

On midsummer's night we built bonfires, reaching high on the hilltops. I looked across from hill to hill, to see the great fires blazing against the scarlet clouds. The black silhouettes of dancers leapt across the flames. We danced through the night, drums pounding, we danced, our voices raised high, we danced, until sweat poured down our sides, we danced, until our sweat

mingled under a vast sea of sky. Later, we lay in the tender summer grass, the shimmering scent of fresh herbs in our hair. We drank the richest wine, ate the sweetest fruits, until the juice stained our lips red. Those were nights to remember. But here you are, the night's chill creeping up your backs, smoke stinging your eyes, in a world slowly falling silent. Can you still hear

the bird's morning songs, bidding plants to grow, the nightly symphony with the bull frog's bass and the tree frog's piccolo? Can you still hear the coyote's chorus under the aspen's stir? All is not lost. Reach out, pick spring's downy leaves, cool round berries, life's lush juice bursting in your hands again. Caress with gentle touch, know our fruit and every seed are one.

About
Return of Bona Dea

Bona Dea was a goddess celebrated by the women of ancient Rome. Revered for her healing powers, her garden temples featured dispensaries for medicinal herbs and treatments for problems related to female fertility. She was often described as the consort of Pan, a deity depicted as half-man, half-goat, and sometimes she was also depicted with horns. In this poem, Bona Dea, the good goddess, returns to our modern world and shares her memories of pagan spring celebrations and a cautionary message regarding our fertility today. Biochemical research has revealed a dangerous, previously unsuspected, relationship between commonly used chemicals and human and animal hormonal systems. Pesticides, plastics, cosmetics, dyes, inks, dry-cleaning solvents, and household cleaning products contain chemicals that mimic or disrupt hormones, the chemically active components of our endocrine systems that control our vital metabolic processes. Our reproductive, immune, and neurological systems are potentially affected by exposure to these endocrine disruptors. The glistening grapes in the illustration, suggests both the use of wine as a path to ecstatic states in ancient festivals celebrating fertility and the current problem of elevated levels of toxic pesticides, herbicides and fungicides often found in commercial grapes.

Breasts

In the café, her breasts rise in tender mounds
quiver like pure joy when she laughs.
Her mouth glints of ruby.

Her fingernails are painted a dark cherry
red wine ripples in her glass
leaving a crimson veil.

She cannot taste the
alchemical brew spiking her drink
or the synthetic venom in her lipstick.

She cannot know what is hidden
in the architecture of her bra,
cannot even remember the cold touch

of solvents on her nails.
Even the air, blue with smoke, quietly betrays her.
She cannot sense these everyday deceptions

or see a ravaged future waiting patiently
by her side. She cannot hear the sad litany
of statistics, cannot see the healers who cut to care.

In the café, her breasts rise in tender mounds
quiver like pure joy when she laughs.
The soft touch of light is her only friend.

About
Breasts

As I sit watching a young woman laughing and talking in a wine bar with her friends, suddenly this happy vision is sadly overtaken by an awareness of the possible invisible threats surrounding us. Along with their wine, these young women are drinking traces of pesticides, herbicides, and fungicides. They are absorbing untested chemicals and materials used to treat and dye their clothing. Their bras may contain polyurethane foam, formaldehyde, and other contaminants. The pesticides and cleaning agents used in this restaurant are finding their way into their bloodstreams. As I sip my own wine, I try to turn away from these troubling thoughts and remember a friend once saying exasperatedly, "Deborah, how can you think about these things all the time?" Later, I thought, "We are the only adults this planet has right now, who else should be thinking about these problems?" The drawing features an alluring glass of wine surrounded by widening circles.

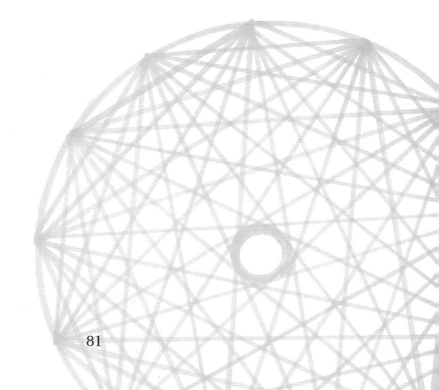

The Cure

Beneath clear skies, striding down the street,
walking women honor missing mothers,
sisters, daughters.
Today, loss stands quietly
on the sidelines.

Search for the Cure, bright banners wave,
stamped with logos, left and right.
Even here cancer stalks two million women
clutches their thin wrists in its iron grip.
No one speaks of the cause
from lips painted
the newest shade,
Baby Blush, Honey Rose,
or Purest Plum.

No one asks about the hidden costs
of each sweet purchase.
No one asks what is the cause
of this tender rot, or
sponsors flee like thieves
running in the night,
dropping bundles
of pink T-shirts.

Beneath clear skies,
flushed faces,
striding down the street,
remember missing mothers,
sisters, daughters.

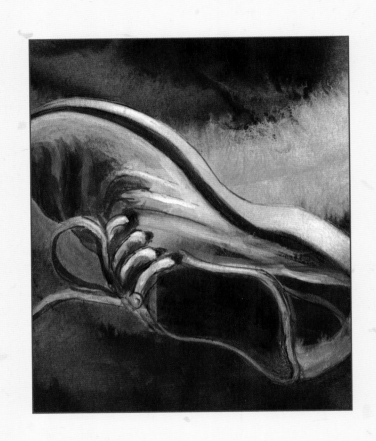

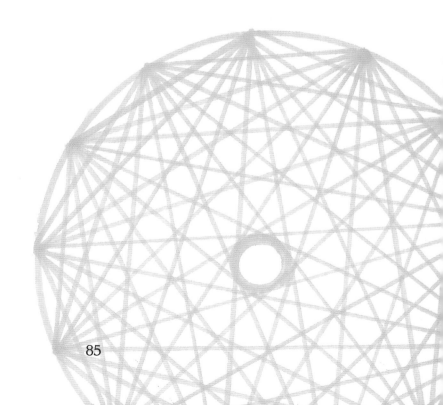

About
The Cure

At a breast cancer run event some years ago, I was impressed by the generous corporate support. Banners and signs emphasized aiding the "search for a cure." After seeing similar events, I started to wonder if their 'ads' were trying to influence the participants. Would these corporate supporters so eagerly sign on to fund a search for the cause of cancer? Probably that research would implicate many of the consumer products they manufacture. The image features a lost running shoe with a background created with a technique called bleeding wet-into-wet. This technique suggests the unseen, fluid movement of toxins through our world.

Chalice

We nursed night and day,
mellow scents filled our pillows
his blue eyes reflecting
this small world.

Breast milk bearing
all the wisdom of our
mothers' and grandmothers'
and great-grandmothers'
bodies, their lifetimes of fighting
insidious invaders.

For one year we nursed,
night and day, cuddled,
sheltered in our nest.
Then he ate from a spoon
and my breasts learned
the pain of making
no more milk.

When my son grew tall
and looked down
to see my face,
I heard bitter news.
Breast milk is now
tainted, hidden poisons
in a mother's gift.

Life's elixir, a
fountain of promise,
thrown upon an altar
piled high with battered
golden chalices.

About Chalice

The year I breastfed my son, I delighted in our loving relationship and being his main source of nourishment. Breast milk is almost miraculously complex and extends many protective health benefits to infants, for example, reduced rates of illnesses, obesity and diabetes. However, now there is a dark side to nursing. A woman's body mobilizes the fats in her body to produce milk. Today, all people's body fats are contaminated by petrochemicals — synthetic chemicals created from petroleum used in consumer goods. As a mother nurses, she "downloads" her chemical "body burden" to her baby along with her milk. This reduces her risk of breast cancer and adds to her child's on-going exposure to chemicals. Sadly, baby formula does not offer a better solution. Tap water, the main ingredient of formula, often contains a brew of chemicals, including rocket fuel, pesticides, and chlorine. The baby formula mixes also are frequently found to be contaminated with heavy metals and BPA, a hormonally active chemical used in plastic production found in the bodies of most people. The artwork depicts a golden chalice with tiny ball and stick drawings of common chemicals below.

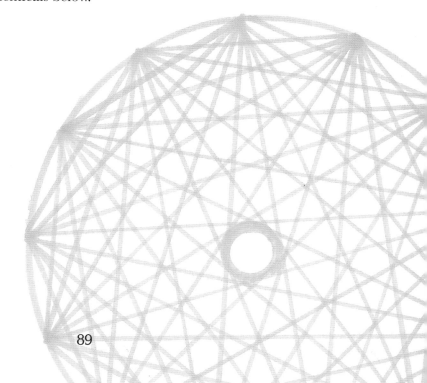

Last Desperate Press

I.

In the beat of time, in the sweep of space, suns circle the reaching void.
Suns so large our entire solar system could turn within their fiery embrace,
even boiling Pluto's blue ice. These massive stars slowly burn every atom,

every shred, explode, implode, flaying molecules a million years away.
Only this titan clash forges the noble metals, platinum, silver, gold
spewing glistening specks to forsaken shoals.

II.

In the beat of time, in the ice of space, our sun's burning, turning potter's wheel
shapes clay and gas. Nine orbs dance to her tune, swinging round in endless revel.
Earth, dressed in lapis blue, deep in her molten magma pools,

liquid granite roils, pushing, lifting mountain masses higher.
Proud quartz and gold hold back clinging together in blazing pits
until the last desperate press they rise, crystal and butter metal

thrust into cracks of grinding granite weaving gold like glittering threads
through mountain's cooling stone. In eon's flux, the Sierra crumbles
precious metal gathers deep like frozen tears in churning river holes.

III.

Gold rushing, gold seething, gold searing. Young men march west
through reckless snow, throbbing with cold and hunger, losing toes
and fingertips. Pale cheeks, raw rough beards in tarnished darkness lie,

hollow eyes roll like stones in the sluice, tracing blighted dreams.
Mining men blast the mountains, rip the roots leave the land barren as the moon,
rivers tainted, to this day with mercury's bitter blessing.

Now, gold wars, edges of machetes catch sunlight in the Congo, gold men scrape deep in earth's black heat. Gold soldiers run, wiry bodies strapped to gold guns. Ancient jeeps careen, wheels spin plumes of dust and dread

over naked, rocky reaches. Cruel harvest for a ring, for a chain.
In the beat of time. In the sweep of space.

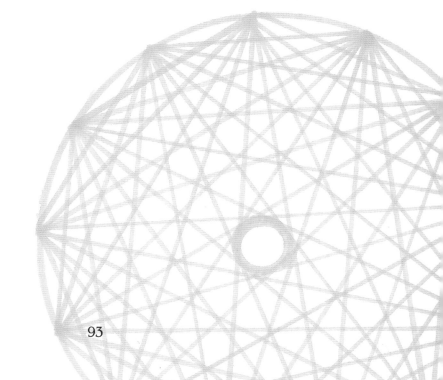

About
Last Desperate Press

Throughout history, humans have valued gold — basing our monetary systems on the precious metal and turning it into objects of great beauty to represent status and power. Despite our fascination with gold, few people are aware of the natural history of this rare metal. Many scientists believe gold molecules only form when an immense sun, whose diameter is larger than our entire solar system, reaches the end of its life and exhausts its nuclear fuel and simultaneously explodes and implodes, transforming into an enormous supernova. Only during these violent cataclysms can the solar nuclear furnaces generate forces intense enough to forge the bonds of noble metals. Unfortunately, today, gold mining and refining is extremely destructive to the environment, degrading habitats and creating persistent contamination of waterways with lead, mercury, and arsenic. The image shows the molecular structure of gold, and its orbiting electrons — also reminiscent of spinning worlds in deep space.

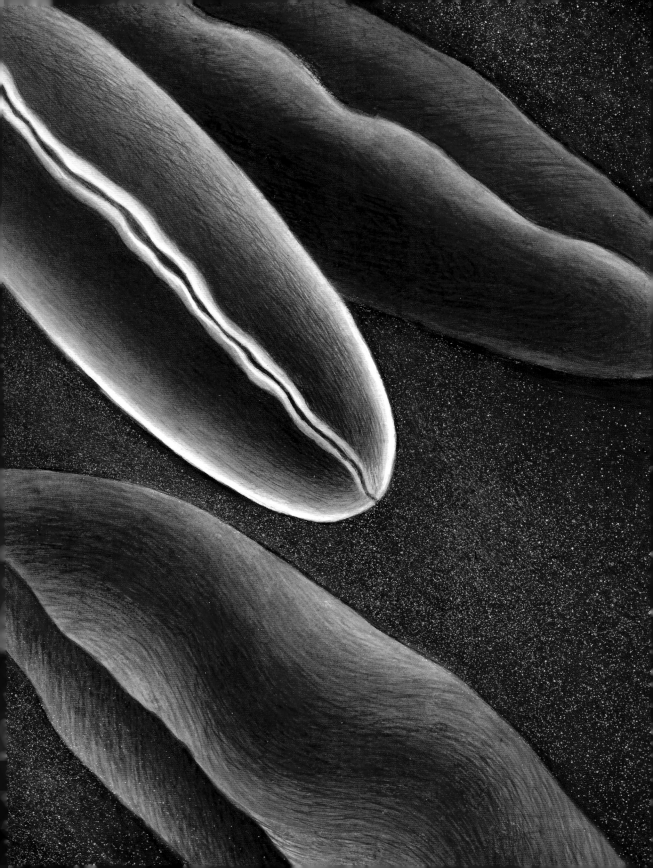

DNA Rules

He is so young, so sharp, does a hundred sit ups while memorizing rows of
Spanish verbs, his head heavy with pros and cons of domestic agrarian policies.
The thick stone walls of his chosen college patiently wait for him to arrive,

bearing suitcases full of plans. He is quicker than a hockey puck, chittering
across the ice, but little blue allergy pills can't stop the nasal pitch in his
voice or the fear of hidden peanuts lurking under his firm grip on reality.

Opening the door, he arrives full of sass, a bounce in every step. My eyes
are blurred and short-sighted after reading endless byzantine posturing in
WHO's "Evaluation of Allergenicity of Genetically Modified Foods."

Visions of transgenic pollen dance like floating shards of glass glinting
in the shafts of sunlight crossing the kitchen. Skimming from the swirling
morass of facts, and half truths I fought through that morning, I ask him

with innocent eyes, "You know why pollen makes your nose drip?"
This morsel of knowledge has escaped the shiny steel trap in his brain, he
shakes his head, a sharp no, laser blue eyes lock on me with a predator's

unnerving stare. I continue, my voice light, "Well, of course, pollen is
the male part of the flower, when it lands on soft damp tissue, it thinks
its found home, sheds its cover, burrows in and starts to fertilize you."

He jerks like a dog, his tender nose just clawed by a cat, "Don't tell me that,
don't tell me that," he yells. But the idea is planted in his head, invisible,
like waves of twisted pollen spilling out of rolling green fields of GMO corn.

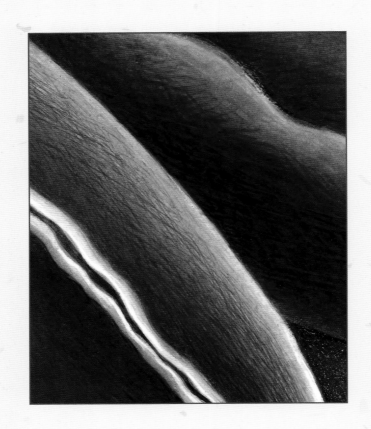

About
DNA Rules

Most people are unaware they are consuming genetically modified organisms (GMOs) in packaged foods every day. The United States, unlike most other developed countries, does not require labeling. The production of this altered food is overseen by The Food and Drug Administration (FDA). Few people realize that the FDA frequently bases claims of GMO safety on unpublished studies conducted by the crop developers themselves. GMO producers promise their modified goods will reduce pesticide use and provide safe, cheap, nutritious food. In fact, GMO crops often require more herbicides and pesticides, and some studies show little evidence of increased crop yield. Studies of GMO-fed animals, usually conducted overseas due to the lack of research in the USA, often reveal dysregulation of immune systems, especially those related to allergy, asthma, and inflammatory conditions. The ink painting features individual pollen grains, the carriers of GMO-altered DNA, magnified by an electron microscope.

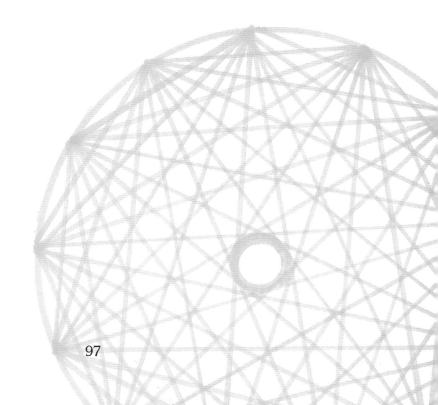

Revealing Relationships
Healing Ourselves and Our Home

"Today we are faced with a challenge that calls for a shift in our thinking, so that humanity stops threatening its life-support system. We are called to assist the Earth to heal her wounds and in the process heal our own — indeed to embrace the whole of creation in all its diversity, beauty and wonder. Recognizing that sustainable development, democracy and peace are indivisible is an idea whose time has come."

WANGARI MAATHAI

More than Light

Wings slice the simmering air
long neck and legs strain forward
each feather burning cold, a shard
of the new moon, taunting noon light.

Egret stands alone, astonished by barren
levees, rubble shaped to shield concrete
carpeted with a poverty of plants.
Beneath my boots the earth still feels

the touch of bare feet, still tastes the brew
of standing water, dark as tea, wetlands
steeping, still longs to bear the weight
of rising ground and lumbering trees.

The earth still hears the rush of a sky
once dark with birds. Sun, fill my eyes
with something more than light.
Count back the searing days

see the endless, indigo nights
listen to forgotten voices. The
young women stand like slender stalks
fires ripple beyond their dance

singing to the bowing oaks, burnished
acorns hanging heavy on every branch.

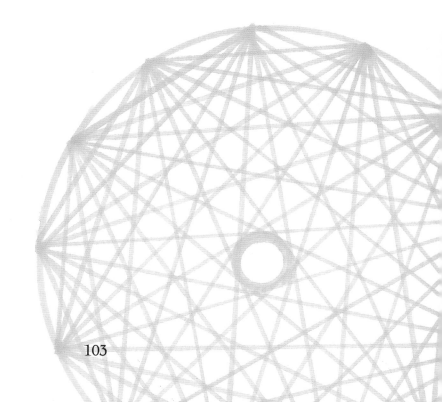

About
More than Light

I frequently explore open areas near my home in the San Francisco Bay Area and then write about my experiences. On this day, I watched an egret land on a levee. Egrets are tall, pristine white birds with graceful curving necks, long legs and beaks. The spare beauty of the egret, so finely shaped, sharpened the contrast with the surrounding brutalized landscape. I began to imagine, as I often do, what this barren environment looked like before Europeans arrived — before Westerners scraped flat the wetlands, and dug the vast salt evaporation ponds. Local precontact lands are described as having very tall, bunch grasses and rich undergrowth covering the wetland areas. Indigenous Ohlone people lived on the high ground, near great stands of ancient oak trees. The Ohlone made their homes and boats of rush, a thick grass reaching thirteen feet tall. They celebrated the powerful oak trees, and their nutritious acorns. During these celebrations, young women sang through the night, their fires dancing, under arching trees and the evening sky. The artwork renders illuminated acorns — the Ohlone's staff of life.

Raise Our Voices

Flying low out of Melbourne, the plane's engines grind
slowly up over miles of bleak baked fields, harvested
down to thin worn threads, a patchwork of dun on dun
all the squares stitched together with curving truck tracks.

A little town crawls below, tiny houses sit in the center
of dark webs as tractors lace together barns and crops.
Beyond this arid outpost, every field is lined with trees like
a neat striped fabric, deep forest green against pale brown.

A bit of wisdom and men's rough hands laid this pattern
leaving bands of trees to shelter the birds, to hold the wet
to bind the soil and defy the gale. Each live leaf reaps
our blazing carbon and bestows the clean gift of breath.

Now, soft, grey green hills rise lightly from parched earth
the forest's tender edge cut straight as a steel razor.
Long ago, the whim of wind and seed set the fate of every tree.
Men map and measure to set the price, inch by inch.

Ridges roll to the horizon, the hills still stand against
eager machines, the land rich with wood and creatures.
But slowly, in the far, fires smolder lazily, gauzy white smoke
curls up to ecru clouds, silent warning of a warming world.

Day by day, each year hotter than the last, fire weather spreads
searing stigmas brand the land, as we strip earth's last green folds.
When the wild winds come, the bush fires burn like blast furnaces
fleeing people, choking, eyes rolling, watch their world turn to dust.

Hear Dreamtime echoes of the First People. *Don't take it all, leave half.*
Tend the trees. Remember, harvesting the earth's ire makes a bitter feast.
Their worn fingers touch the living fibers binding the rocks, the water,
the air, voices ripple in the night, calling, calling, bring back the rain.

About
Raise Our Voices

As I flew out of Melbourne I saw the evidence of prolonged drought and a warming climate: parched land with numerous bush fires burning in the distance. Miles of roads, fences and dry fields slipped below me. I remembered seeing an Australian documentary with an aboriginal man harvesting turtle eggs, a delicacy of his people. He said, "Don't take them all, leave half." His essential knowledge — not to take everything — would be a wise guideline for all people and societies today and could help slow many of our looming environmental problems. The illustration depicts what is called by contemporary Australians a "scar tree." These trees carved by the First Peoples of Australia had spiritual significance and still stand in the fields and forests "down under."

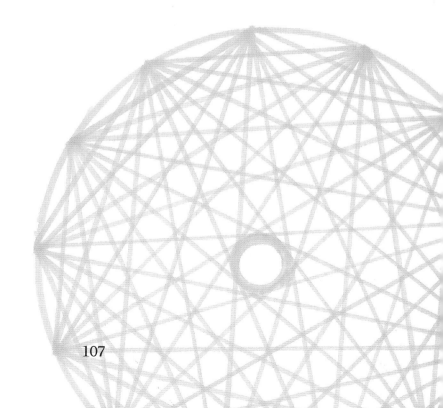

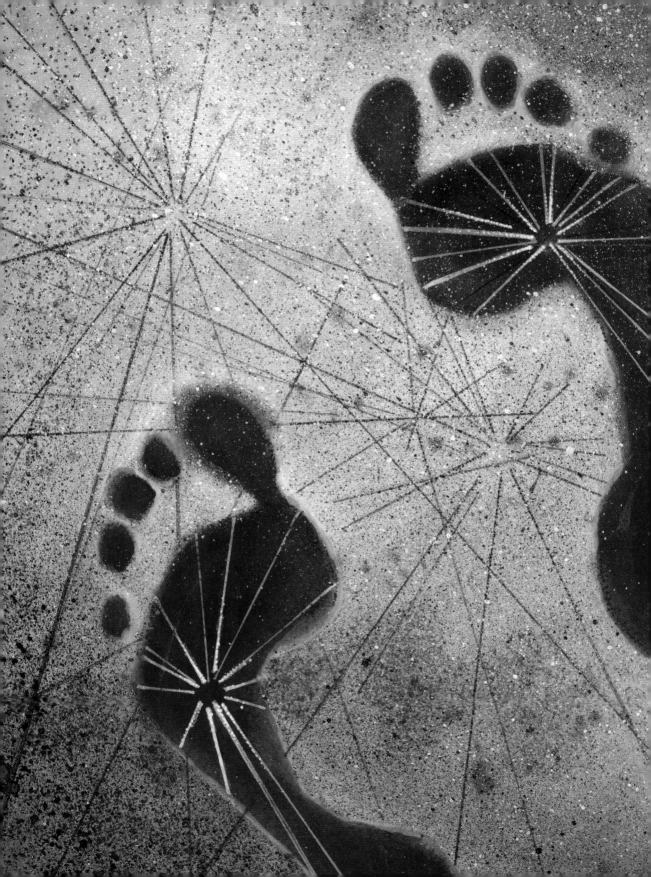

The Beaten Path

Hiking up St. Joe's hill, underfoot a rutted road
shallow channels cut by winter runoff, knobby stones
and satin serpentine brought to light after an eon's burial.
Mountain bikers, pass on the left, heavy tires grind

against the grade. Below, cars flow by, nestled deep in
the San Andreas Fault, like leaves slipping down a dark river.
On this side of the hill the valley stretches to the bay
trees give way to buildings hung in a sullen haze.

On the other side, a half-drained reservoir and scrubby hills
growing back from last year's fire. Native people
made this trail, following the hill's broad shoulder.
Like their distant cousins, in Peru, etching the Nazca lines

tracing sacred geometry across thin, high-desert soil.
Beneath the lines, the earth is dense as rammed earth floors.
Each pebble remembers the slow rhythms, the stamping feet
of the people praying for rain, slowly shaping buried trails

only satellites can see. The beaten path beneath my feet
once followed by first people through turning seasons.
They travelled from a different valley, wet and verdant
thrumming with beating wings, walking with eager feet

bound for a coast roiling with succulent fish. Raising my head
the hill's bleached grass smolders with fiery light, the ghost
of fires set long ago by Mexican rancheros, their calloused
hands slashed and burned breathing trees to feed their cattle.

Across the valley, my enamel eyes see each building slowly
crumble, leaving only sloping mounds carpeted with acid
yellow flowers. Turning back, my pilgrim's trail wanders
down through silent ravines echoing with night's blue air.

About
The Beaten Path

Reading Gary Nabhan's book of essays, *Cultures of Habitat: On Nature, Culture and Story*, still affects me, helping me see the living history in the land around me. In this book, Nabhan travels the American West and writes movingly about lost Native American communities and their enduring impact on the local ecology. Through his studies he discovers greater biodiversity in places where populations are most stable. Communities living for long times in specific habitats usually discover successful ways of fostering the local wildlife. Conversely, areas of frequent migrations tend to lead to more endangered plants and animals. His work helped me see the enduring impact of early people on the land around me. The illustration features footprints and the patterns of radiating lines derived from the designs created by the Nazca people who lived in Peru from 1100 BCE to 750 CE. They are best known for the Nazca lines, or geoglyphs — designs inscribed in the desert soil. The lines frequently depict animals and birds, as well as geometric forms and are many miles long. Recently, German scientists used satellites to analyze these geoglyphs and found deep compression of the soil under some lines. They theorize that the ancient people may have walked or danced across the lines while performing religious ceremonies, slowly creating densely compacted areas over many decades.

Two Halves of the Story

For I.R.G.

Ago, we say, long ago, even long, long
ago, we told tales by the fire, our eyes bright
whispering the stories, how the world was born and
how its two sides fit together like halves of a clamshell.

Binding curves embrace every desire
to love, to birth, to care, to hold
to peel the vegetables and light the fire.
Binding curves embrace every desire
to take, to tear, to grip the blade, knuckles white
bullwhips hanging in calloused fists.

Two halves of the story
two halves of our hands
plus one half of the tools
and one half of the weapons.

Each side filled with stories, coiled strings of cloudy pearls.
Hear their half, shrouded in dark details — the raging fevers
the lost lands, The Bloody Trail. He tells me his grandmother
walked that cruel path, but she was strong and walked on
as others fell. So now he stands by an empty lighthouse
watching, waiting to see the rivers run red with salmon again.

The other half of the story is hardly ever told
and all the details moulder under stacks of tall tales.
A few persistent specters, poking in piles of old papers
turning to dirt on floors of locked sheds, still know.

Could the world once been round like a fresh picked apple
without a single bite taken and all the stories fit together
in one song and every night they sang together
and the wind blew all their words up to the mountains?

Or perhaps, the world was never round, the stories were never sung and the words always burned to white ash in the fire.

Two halves of the story
two halves of our hands
one half of the weapons
one half of the tools.

About
Two Halves of the Story

Last summer on a road trip with my husband, we drove up the California coast. At a scenic overlook I encountered a young man from the local Pomo tribe. As we talked, a breeze swept over the shimmering coastline. In the cove below, his people had harvested abalone for their iridescent shells and tender meat. I imagined their graceful, sea-faring boats made of tule or long rushes floating in the churning water, their children excitedly shouting with delight as they swam in the cold ocean waves. Now this area is a preserve, where visitors stroll on the cliffs, and all fishing is forbidden. The young Pomo man told me stories from his family history, and the trials visited on his people — the waves of epidemics, the raids of slavers and being uprooted and confined to a reservation. His grandmother was a valiant survivor of the Bloody Trail, a punishing forced march from Fort Bragg inflicted on the Pomo; these stories inspired this poem. The image suggests the poem's metaphor of the two sides of the world fitting together like halves of a clamshell — an idea echoed from myths of Pacific Islanders and Pacific Northwest indigenous peoples.

Native

I.

Digging dirt in my backyard, heavy, dark dirt, dried so hard
it makes my pickaxe sing. Turning, I look for what has lasted here
besides this mute soil. What has endured from long before,
the bacterial assault carried by men bearing the white man's burden,
the quiet corruption that burned away so many who once walked this land.

Before the tender mercy of the Missions blessed so many more
with early graves before the last, red wave of manifest destiny.
Only this coast live oak, reaching skyward for two hundred years,
remains. Heavy limbs stripping wind from sky, coiling roots gripping earth,
a native plant, belonging to this reluctant rain and this scorched soil.

II.

Today, my neighbor dug a hole for a Japanese maple dressed in
fine russet leaves. Shovel driving down in hard ground, he heard
a hollow tone, struck a skull in his yard, buried five hundred years.
He said, "Put it in a graveyard." My feet sink in loose warm soil,
the graveyard is here, sacred earth consecrated for all time.

Here was a family, a fire ring, and here was a home built of tule grass.
My shovel pries a clod of caked clay. I beat the tangled, white roots
of Bermuda grass, breaking dry dirt from reaching rhizomes. Once
this soil held only plants named in native tongues. Yet, this earth
does not spurn the grasping roots of foreign bushes ringing my backyard.
Heavenly bamboo, tough as stone in months of heat, Australian

bottlebrush, red flowers humming with ardent bees, sour tangerines
from Morocco's plains blackened by this valley's somber air.
I drive my shovel into the ground, grip weathered wood like a staff.
In the sky, bleached by summer heat, tiny fighters spar with fierce precision.
Hummingbirds defend beads of nectar crowning my Mexican sage.

Sun sears my thin hair, sweat beads across my faint cheeks.
Slowly, I breathe in dusty air and breathe out a silent plea, dark dirt,
let my wandering feet belong to you, be my house, be my home.

About
Native

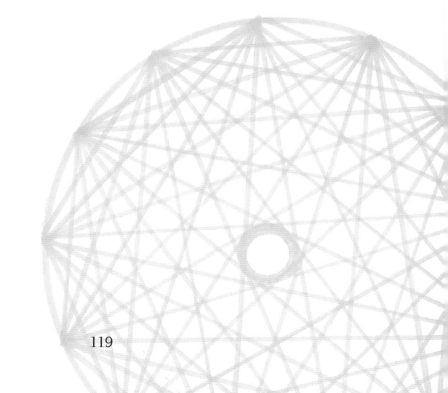

Just over two hundred years ago, undisturbed Native American communities thrived in the area called California today. These flourishing peoples of the West Coast spoke one hundred different languages, and belonged to at least five hundred subtribes suggesting a remarkable level of tolerance and cooperation. Acorns were a staple crop, but they also ate a wide variety of foods, including roots, fruits, seeds, birds, fish, deer, and antelope. Sadly, the diseases brought by white explorers killed an estimated ninety percent of the indigenous peoples in the Americas. White settlers often discovered a beautiful "wilderness," without realizing that the land had only recently been emptied of native communities. Can I, a transplant from three thousand miles away, and an inheritor of such dark history, ever belong deeply to this place, I call home? The drawing includes the leaves from a native Coast Live Oak from my backyard and a human skull.

Metronome

Metronome in my chest
measures the minutes
measures the seconds
more than half gone now.

This pump, a crimson miracle
beating quietly
for fifty-five years.

My father's heart rebelled
this doubled year.
In the darkness
the pressure of blood beats

against my eardrums.
My eyes see the glow
of waiting machines.
Outside, a mockingbird sings

under a sliver of moon.
The old moon
in the new moon's arms

thin arc of ardent light
embraces her faint
round face.

The mockingbird's razor notes
pierce my empty yard.
His song reaches

for reckless registers,
rips through antic rhythms.

The wind surges through
trees etched against the
indigo sky. This bird's heart

beats so fast, my seconds
are as long as lightyears.

About
Metronome

My father and older sister had violent encounters with heart disease at age fifty-five. When I reached this age, I would lie in bed wondering whether a similar fate awaited me. It was a very long year. While worry weighed heavily on my chest, I listened to the nighttime songs of the mockingbirds. As their name implies, mockingbirds imitate the calls of other birds, and now they even imitate car alarms and ringing telephones. The males can learn up to two hundred songs and their vocal gymnastics, intended to assert territorial claims and attract females, are vibrant and extravagant. As those difficult nights unfolded for me, the mockingbird's proud repertoire of songs gave me new heart and hope. The image is of a saucy mockingbird perched near my heart.

White Violets

Dirt road rakes up the valley,
mercifully graded
not for my bike
but for rumbling logging trucks
long gone.
Still woodland, jade in early light,
all young trees grown

from a fallen forest.
Handlebars jerk left and right,
my legs pump up the slow hill,
pushing in low gear.
Stopping, leaning into the frame,
blowing like a horse
on a first spring ride.
Sound streams skyward,

a wood thrush call swells up,
spiral flute, wellspring rising.
Sun sifts through
ten thousand leaves,
redwood and madrone,
raucous revival
of every stained glass green.
At my feet, white violets
dance like tiny angels

on the point of a pin.
The thrush's ice clear call
circles through dusty shadows.
Each note, memory's spur.

About
White Violets

I heard the call of a wood thrush for the first time forty years ago. Standing in a hot, steamy New Hampshire forest, harried on all sides by clouds of mosquitoes, I was suddenly transfixed by a soaring wood thrush song. I am still enchanted by their music and treasure the times I hear them sing. With their extraordinary double voice boxes, they create rippling, flute-like songs. Birders often describe their song as the most beautiful of all North American birds. Although not a threatened species, the thrush population is declining, as are those of many songbirds. Most people have felt the power of human music to unleash emotions, but more rarely sense the impact of the natural world's sounds on the deeper parts of ourselves.

Redwoods

Circling like Matisse's dancers,
tender saplings rolling round.
Boughs reach to distant dome,
soft tips barely brush sixty feet.

In the center of the center,
specter of the mother tree.
So long lost, not even a stump
stands like a black and broken tooth,
only a ring of young clones
trace the edge of her faded footprint.

For two thousand years
this unyielding pillar's will
tamed the burning winds.
Each fine leaf winnowed fog
until virgin water dripped down
bringing life to land and creek.

The last great steward of this land
until two loggers, thin as razors,
Left Chopper and Right Chopper,
rained down blows, and the rise and fall
of double-bite axes split the forest day by day,
week by week. They dropped her down,
a shattered world, like Rome's fall
to empty men gripping sacks of hunger.

One memory remains, a sepia photograph,
the whole logging camp and one bored mule,
standing on the broken trunk,
proud conquerors on a massive prow.

Now, fog hangs like tattered lace along the coast.
This living palisade bars the blistering sun,
casting shadows rich with reverie.
Sunbeams slip into the dusk, prisms blind
with future sight as centuries turn by the score.
In that time, in that place, this one great
redwood stands and rules the land again.

About
Redwoods

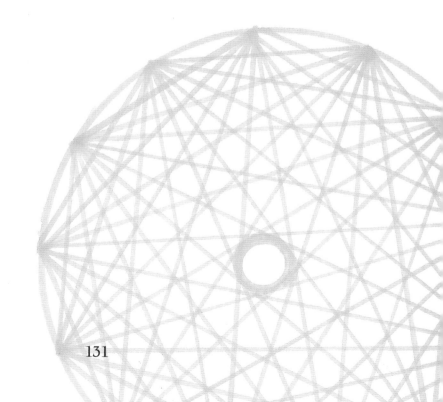

Last summer, on a hike in the hills near Santa Cruz, California, I discovered graceful circles of redwood trees. These rings of young trees are descendants of great trees often felled long ago. The "mother" trees had burls at their bases — ring collars containing innumerable dormant sprouts. When the old trees were downed, new trees sprung up from the burls on the circular footprints of the lost trees. These young trees perfectly replicate the ancient genetic material of the mother trees which can be eight hundred to two thousand years old. Since the California Gold Rush in the 1800s loggers have cut down ninety-six percent of redwood forests. Today, legal logging and dangerous levels of poaching continue to diminish redwood stands. Activists call for enforcement of a Zero Cut policy to preserve what remains of these increasingly rare trees. The image shows part of a family circle of young redwood trees and reveals how they create their own climates — damp and cool — with the sun's light barely piercing their shadows.

Fate of My Son

I.

Slicing harvest squash, forcing the slender blade through hard
pith. This knife was forged by men breathing sulfur, coal dust

in every pore. After the Civil War, they stopped making scores
of Yankee swords and made this kitchen knife. A man

with steady hands watched the steel turn cherry red in the fire
then hammered until it cooled. The fine edge cuts through carrots

like a spoon through ripe avocado. Mincing polished cloves
of garlic, bracing my fingers against the tapered spine,

my thin skin, cool against the metal. A little stream of fear
flows to a deeper well, hidden in a hollow, just below my ribs.

Memories float to the top of this still water. I walk through
a marsh, blazing in the bleached light of the waxing moon.

II.

The world is a half cup of cold tea sitting in the kitchen sink.
Each of my son's minutes tip on a scale, every word

weighed against the last. A slip of water chants quietly
to the moon, the cattails etch black letters on silver ripples.

I read every sign, begging for a prophet's feral eyes.
Each moment hangs like a Damascus steel sword

held by a ribbon cut from clouds. The wind spins around me
a simmering broth scented with fresh herbs. A mourning dove

circles, her call rising and falling, turns to steel in the marrow of my bones. The stars stop, the center of the sun is still.

As the bird settles to its roost, every domino of his life tips over one after another chasing each other across the polished floor.

About
Fate of My Son

Parents and children naturally share an intense, caring emotional bond. As parents, we try to provide our children with all they need, including emotional support, interesting experiences, challenging educations and material goods. In developed countries this caring can translate into shopping for overwhelming amounts of clothes, shoes, car carriers, travel strollers, plastic toys, sports equipment, tech toys, books, smart phones, and computers. All these goods must be repeatedly replaced as the child grows older. We work and shop, trying to be good parents. However, our caring efforts often starkly contrast with our lack of mindful attention to the source of these goods — the larger natural world. Humans, like all species, require functioning habitats. We cannot nurture our children now or in the future without a healthy thriving planet. Perhaps what our children really need most is much greater caring and protection for our planet. The artwork depicts a flying mourning dove in a complex environment.

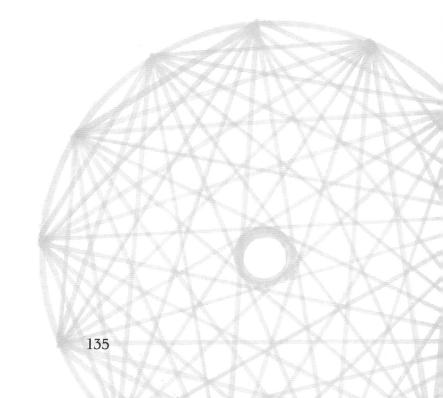

Regeneration Ruckus

Cypress Pond — written in brown ink with a lovely looping hand on the 1807
field notes of the General Land Office — marks the last fingerprint of the Mississippi
River pressed into the yielding soil of southern Illinois. The First People gave
this swamp to herons and hawks, but by 1900, brash young men ready to squeeze

the juice from this fresh world, felled the trees, drained the dark, still water and
planted row crops — corn for the cows. Then dry years came, and wildfires burned
hot and fast. After the war, everyone just lost interest and left it be. All alone,
the second-growth trees slowly tried to remember what it was they meant to say.

In 1960, the patient men at State Fish and Game knitted together all the wandering
water of that ancient swamp into one small lake, flat and blue as an afghan on a sofa.
They built tidy blinds where the hunters crouch in the sharp bite of daybreak's chill
waiting, waiting to shoot a duck and feel the grit men once carried in their bones.

This stretch of Massac County, still dotted with small farms, quietly spun through
the seasons until May 6, 2003, an F4 hit, sudden, hard, a bolt from above, the winds
beyond wind ground through the forest's careless order, left behind an unholy mess.
Soon, the loggers roared through this shell-shocked land with feller bunchers and

grapple skidders as they tenderly hauled out all the blow-down trees set for the sawmill.
In the slash, left by the buckers and windthrow, the foresters arrived to count every tree
still left — stump, standing or topped. They carefully marked their grids, added the
numbers and shrewdly concluded — repeated disturbances hasten ecological surprises.

Now, the Buckeyes, Sassafras and Swamp Ash, are belting out hot new songs
saplings bursting up from every stump and frowzy shrubs are running riot
in the skid tracks. Each thicket pulses with the beat of nature's deep redemption —
grant the smallest claim and the force of nature blasts back with lusty new rhythms.

About
Regeneration Ruckus

In December 2013 I was crossing the street, and two cars stopped for me at the crosswalk. Suddenly a car coming from the opposite direction, hit me at over thirty miles per hour. Both my legs and eight other bones were broken, and my brain suffered a traumatic injury. Now I can walk well (except for stairs and hills) and am teaching and working again as an artist and writer. Through this harrowing experience, I gained new appreciation for the extraordinary power of regeneration. Just as the human body can rebound from serious injuries, the natural world repeatedly proves that if we protect and restore natural areas, its communities of plants and animals will explosively repopulate. The artwork records a powerful F4 tornado tearing through a forest with teasels, very resilient field plants, in the foreground.

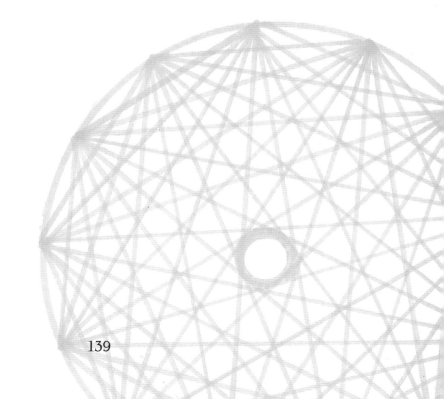

References

Living inside the Circle: Every Part Wedded to the Whole

Coevolution

Hone, Dave. "Moth tongues, orchids and Darwin – the predictive power of evolution." *The Guardian*. (2013). https://www.theguardian.com/science/lost-worlds/2013/oct/02/moth-tongues-orchids-darwin-evolution (accessed July 24, 2016).

Kritsky, Gene. "Darwin's Madagascan Hawk Moth Prediction." *American Entomologist* 37, no. 4 (1991). 206-210, http://dx.doi.org/10.1093/ae/37.4.206 (accessed July 26, 2014).

Web of Life

Billings, W. D. "The Environmental Complex in Relation to Plant Growth and Distribution." *The Quarterly Review of Biology* 27, no. 3 (1952): 251-265.

Capra, Fritjof. *The Web of Life: A New Scientific Understanding of Living Systems*. New York: Anchor Books, 1997.

Double Vision

Berry, Thomas. *The Dream of the Earth*. San Francisco: Sierra Club Books, 1988, 131.

Atmospheric Optics. "Ice Crystal Halos." http://www.atoptics.co.uk/halosim.htm (accessed April 29, 2016).

Sign Language

International Chicken Genome Sequencing Consortium. "Sequence and Comparative Analysis of the Chicken Genome Provide Unique Perspectives on Vertebrate Evolution." *Nature* 432 (2004): 695-716. doi:10.1038/nature03154 (accessed July 14, 2016).

Bone Shadows

Bingham, Ann. *South and Meso-American Mythology, A to Z*. New York: Chelsea House, 2010, 126.

Boone, Elizabeth Hill. *The Art and Iconography of Late Post-Classic Central Mexico*. Washington, DC: Dumbarton Oaks Trustees, 1982, 7.

Rough-legged Hawk

U.S. Fish and Wildlife Service Division of Migratory Bird Management. "Raptors: Diurnal and Nocturnal Birds of Prey." *US Fish & Wildlife Publications* (2002). University of

Nebraska, Lincoln. http://digitalcommons.unl.edu/usfwspubs/384/ (accessed April 29, 2016).

Convention on the Conservation of Migratory Species of Wild Animals. "Birds of Prey (Raptors)." http://www.cms.int/en/legalinstrument/birds-prey-raptors (accessed May 5, 2013).

Sweet Water to Salt

US Environmental Protection Agency. "Introduction to Watershed Ecology." https://cfpub.epa.gov/watertrain/moduleFrame.cfm?parent_object_id=518 (accessed April 29, 2016).

Careless Hands: Wreaking and Reaping

Teeming

Hornaday, William Temple. "The Extermination of the American Bison." *The Evolution of the Conservation Movement, 1850-1920* (1889): 387-393. http://memory.loc.gov/cgi-bin/query/r?ammem/consrv:@field(DOCID+@lit(amrvrvr02div11)) (accessed June 30, 2016).

Johns, Joshua. "Nature and the American Identity: A Brief History of Nature and the American Consciousness." http://xroads.virginia.edu/~cap/nature/cap2.html (accessed March 3, 2013).

Quorum Sensing

Audubon. "The Extinction of the Great Auk." http://johnjames.audubon.org/extinction-great-auk (accessed April 29, 2016).

Klappenback, Laura. "Things You Can Do to Protect Wildlife." *About.com.* http://animals.about.com/od/wildlifeconservation/tp/helping_endangered_species.htm (accessed July 10, 2016).

Twigger, Robert. "Bird Extinctions May Hold Clues to Human Survival." London: *The Independent* (2001). *National Geographic News*, last modified October 28, 2010. http://news.nationalgeographic.com/news/2001/07/0727_wiretwigger.html (accessed February 7, 2016.

Gilt Frames

Center for Biological Diversity. "Court Upholds Endangered Species Act Protection for Polar Bears." Press release, June 30, 2011. http://www.biologicaldiversity.org/news/press_releases/2011/polar-bear-06-30-2011.html (accessed July 14, 2016).

Friel, Howard. *The Lomborg Deception: Setting the Record Straight about Global Warming.* New Haven: Yale University Press, 2010.

Klein, Naomi. *This Changes Everything: Capitalism vs. The Climate.* New York: Simon & Schuster, 2015.

Roach, John. "Most Polar Bears Gone By 2050, Studies Say." *National Geographic News* (2007), last modified October 28, 2010. http://news.nationalgeographic.com/news/2007/09/070910-polar-bears.html (accessed July 20, 2016).

Midnight Garden

Thomas, C. D. and J. C. G. Abery. "Estimating Rates of Butterfly Decline from Distribution Maps: The Effect of Scale." *Biological Conservation* 73, no.1 (1995): 59–65. doi:10.1016/0006-3207(95)90065-9 (accessed July 7, 2016).

Paper Wings

Butcher, Greg. "Common Birds in Decline." *A State of the Birds Report.* Aubudon (2007). http://www.audubon.org/sites/default/files/documents/sotb_cbid_magazine.pdf (accessed July 22, 2016).

Ottinger, Mary Ann, Emma T. Lavoie, Mahmoud Abdelnabi, Michale J. Quinn Jr., Allegra Marcell, and Karen Dean. "An Overview of Dioxin-Like Compounds, PCB, and Pesticide Exposures Associated with Sexual Differentiation of Neuroendocrine Systems, Fluctuating Asymmetry, and Behavioral Effects in Birds." *Journal of Environmental Science and Health, Part C: Environmental Carcinogenesis and Ecotoxicology Reviews* 27, no. 4 (2009): 286-300. doi: 10.1080/10590500903310229.

Mehlman, David. *The Nature Conservancy*. "The 2011 State of the Birds Report." http://blog.nature.org/conservancy/2011/05/03/the-2011-state-of-the-birds-report/ (accessed July 10, 2016).

Vacation Apocalypse

Worthy, Kenneth. *Invisible Nature: Healing the Destructive Divide between People and the Environment.* Amherst, MA: Prometheus Books, 2013, 17.

Hole Minus Hole

Carson, Rachel. *Silent Spring.* Boston: Houghton Mifflin, 1962, 277.
Vice. Shane Smith. "Greenland is Melting & Bonded Labor." *HBO,* March 21, 2014.

La Femme Savant

Oreskes, Naomi and Erik M. Conway. *Merchants of Doubt: How a Handful of Scientists Obscured the Truth on Issues from Tobacco Smoke to Global Warming.* New York: Bloomsbury Press, 2011.

Beautiful Poisons: Bearing the Burden

Secrets

Dunagan, Sarah C., Robin E. Dodson, Ruthann A. Rudel, and Julia G. Brody. "Toxics Use Reduction in the Home: Lessons Learned from Household Exposure Studies." *Journal of Cleaner Production* 19, no. 5 (2011): 438-444. doi: 10.1016/j.jclepro.2010.06.012 (accessed July 23, 2016).

Environmental Working Group. "Body Burden: The Pollution in Newborns." Last modified July 14, 2005. http://www.ewg.org/research/body-burden-pollution-newborns (accessed July 20, 2016).

Loukmas, Heather, Stephen Boese, and Marianne McCoy. "Unwanted Exposure: Preventing Environmental Threats to the Health of New York State's Children." Healthy Schools Network, Inc. and Learning Disabilities Association of New York State (2007). http://www.healthyschools.org/downloads/Unwanted_Exposure_Report.pdf (accessed July 20, 2016).

Steinbraber, Sandra. *Living Downstream: An Ecologist's Personal Investigation of Cancer and the Environment*. Cambridge, MA: Da Capo Press, 2010.

Trasande, Leonardo and Yinghua Liu. "Reducing the Staggering Costs of Environmental Disease in Children, Estimated at $76.6 Billion in 2008." *Health Affairs* (2011). doi: 10.1377/hlthaff.2010.1239 (accessed July 25, 2016).

Vogel, Sarah A. and Jody A. Roberts. "Why The Toxic Substances Control Act Needs an Overhaul, And How to Strengthen Oversight of Chemicals in the Interim." *Health Affairs* 30, no. 5 (2011): 898-905. doi: 10.1377/hlthaff.2011.0211 (accessed July 26, 2016).

The Return of Bona Dea

Colborn, Theo, Dianne Dumanoski, and John Peterson Myers. *Our Stolen Future: Are We Threatening Our Fertility, Intelligence, and Survival? A Scientific Detective Story.* New York: Dutton, 1996.

Mayo Clinic Staff. "Diseases and Conditions: Male Infertility." Last modified August 11, 2015. http://www.mayoclinic.org/diseases-conditions/male-infertility/basics/causes/con-20033113 (accessed July 25, 2016).

Oliva, Alejandro, Alfred Spira, and Luc Multigner. "Contribution of Environmental Factors to the Risk of Male Infertility." *Human Reproduction* 16, no. 8 (2001): 1768-776. doi: 10.1093/humrep/16.8.1768 (accessed July 15, 2016).

Toxics Action Center. "The Problem with Pesticides." http://www.toxicsaction.org/problems-and-solutions/pesticides (accessed April 30, 2016).

Breasts

Brody, Julia G. "Everyday Exposures and Breast Cancer." *Reviews on Environmental Health* 25, no. 1 (2010). http://silentspring.org/sites/default/files/01-REH25%281%292010Brody.pdf (accessed May 1, 2016).

Clement, Brian and Anne Marie. *Killer Clothes: How Seemingly Innocent Clothing Choices Endanger Your Health . . . and how to protect yourself!* Las Vegas: Hippocrates Publications, 2011.

Smith, Rick, Bruce Lourie, and Sarah Dopp. *Slow Death by Rubber Duck: How the Toxic Chemistry of Everyday Life Affects Our Health.* Toronto: Knopf Canada, 2009.

Stockholm University. "Stain- and waterproof clothing are harmful." Last modified May 18, 2015. http://www.su.se/english/about/profile-areas/climate-seas-and-environment/stain-and-waterproof-clothing-are-harmful-1.236470 (accessed May 14, 2016).

Doheny, Kathleen. "Is Your Nail Polish Toxic?" *WebMD Health News*. Last modified April 11, 2012. http://www.webmd.com/beauty/nails/20120411/is-your-nail-polish-toxic (accessed April 5, 2016).

Breast Cancer. "Exposure to Chemicals in Cosmetics." http://www.breastcancer.org/risk/factors/cosmetics (accessed April 29, 2016).

The Cure

Love, Susan. "Real Race in Cancer is Finding Its Cause." *The New York Times*, February 6, 2012. http://www.nytimes.com/2012/02/07/health/breast-cancer-screening-matters-but-prevention-is-the-real-goal.html?_r=0 (accessed May 10, 2016).

Sulik, Gail. *Pink Ribbon Blues: How Breast Cancer Culture Undermines Women's Health*. Cary, NC: Oxford University Press, 2012.

Williams, Florence. *Breasts: A Natural and Unnatural History*. New York: W.W. Norton & Co., 2012.

Chalice

Environmental Working Group. "Moms and Pops: Persistent Organic Pollutants in the diets of pregnant and nursing women." Last modified March 1, 2000. http://www.ewg.org/research/moms-and-pops (accessed June 20, 2016).

Limbach, James. "Infant Formula Recalls." *Consumer Affairs*. June 9, 2014. https://www.consumeraffairs.com/infant-formula-recalls (accessed May 29, 2016).

Last Desperate Press

New World Encyclopedia. "Sierra Nevada (U.S.)." Last modified September 17, 2015. http://www.newworldencyclopedia.org/entry/Sierra_Nevada_(U.S.) (accessed July 10, 2016).

Smith, Michelle. "Gold Mining in Africa: The Need for Corporate Social Responsibility." *Gold Investing News*. November 17, 2011. http://investingnews.com/daily/resource-investing/precious-metals-investing/gold-investing/gold-mining-in-africa-the-need-for-corporate-social-responsibility/ (accessed July 20, 2016).

DNA Rules

FDA. "FDA's Role in Regulating Safety of GE Foods." *FDA Consumer Health Information*, May 2013. https://njfb.org/wp-content/uploads/2013/07/FDA-GE-Answers.pdf (accessed July 23, 2016).

Hilbeck, Angelika, et al. "No Scientific Consensus on GMO Safety." *Environmental Sciences Europe* 27, no. 4 (2015). doi: 10.1186/s12302-014-0034-1 (accessed July 26, 2016).

Amos, Brit. "Death of the Bees. Genetically Modified Crops and the Decline of Bee Colonies in North America." *Global Research*. August 9, 2011. http://www.globalresearch.ca/death-of-the-bees-genetically-modified-crops-and-the-decline-of-bee-colonies-in-north-america/25950 (accessed July 16, 2016).

Revealing Relationships: Healing Ourselves and Our Home

More than Light

Margolin, Malcolm. *The Ohlone Way: Indian Life in the San Francisco-Monterey Bay Area.* Berkeley: Heyday Press, 1978.

Castillo, Edward D. "Short Overview of California Indian History." *California Native American Heritage Commission.* http://nahc.ca.gov/resources/california-indian-history/ (accessed April 30, 2016).

Raise Our Voices

Unesco. "Best Practices on Indigenous Knowledge." *Management of Social Transformations Programme and The Centre for International Research and Advisory Netwroks.* http://www.unesco.org/most/bpikpub.htm (accessed April 30, 2016).

The Beaten Path

Geddes, Linda. "Peruvians walked their prayers into the earth." *New Scientist: Histories,* January 21, 2009. https://www.newscientist.com/article/mg20126924-200-peruvians-walked-their-prayers-into-the-earth/ (accessed April 15, 2016).

Hall, Stephen S. "Spirits in the Sand." *National Geographic.* March 2010. http://ngm.nationalgeographic.com/print/2010/03/nasca/hall-text (accessed July 1, 2016).

Two Halves of the Story

Castillo, Elias. *A Cross of Thorns: The Enslavement of California's Indians by the Spanish Missions.* Fresno, CA: Craven Street Books, 2015.

Gelles, Paul H. *Chumash Renaissance: Indian Casinos, Education and Cultural Politics in Rural California.* Santa Barbara, CA: Solitude Canyon Press, 2013.

Native

Gomez-Pena, Guillermo. *The New World Border: Prophecies, Poems, and Loqueras for the End of the Century.* San Francisco: City Lights Publishers, 2001.

Kincheloe, John W., III. "American Indians at European Contact." *Tar Heel Junior Historian 47, no. 1* (2007). http://ncpedia.org/history/early/contact (accessed July 25, 2016).

Loewen, James W. *Lies My Teacher Told Me: Everything Your American History Textbook Got Wrong.* New York: Touchstone, 2007.

Nabban, Gary P. *Cultures of Habitat: On Nature, Culture, and Story.* Berkeley: Counterpoint Press, 1998.

Metronome

All About Birds. "Northern Mockingbird." *The Cornell Lab of Ornithology.* 2016. https://www.allaboutbirds.org/guide/Northern_Mockingbird/id (accessed April 29, 2016).

White Violets

All About Birds. "Swainson's Thrush." *The Cornell Lab of Ornithology.* https://www.allaboutbirds.org/guide/Swainsons_Thrush/id (accessed April 29, 2016).

Redwoods

Kauchik, "The Lumberjacks Who Felled California's Giant Redwoods." *Amusing Planet.* October 19, 2012. http://www.amusingplanet.com/2012/10/the-lumberjacks-who-felled-californias.html (accessed April 29, 2016).

National Park Service. "Redwood." https://www.nps.gov/redw/faqs.htm#__topdoc__ (accessed June 24, 2016).

Fate of My Son

Rosenbaum, Sara and Robert Blum. "How Healthy Are Our Children?" *The Future of Children 25, no. 1* (2015): 11-34. http://www.futureofchildren.org/publications/docs/25_1_chapter%201.pdf (accessed April 30, 2016).

Regeneration Ruckus

National Weather Service. "May 6, 2003 Tornado Outbreak." http://www.weather.gov/media/pah/Top10Events/2003/May6.pdf (accessed April 30, 2016).

Environmental Organizations and Resources

For further reading on these subjects visit:

Alliance for Zero Extinction
ZeroExtinction.org
Pinpoint and conserve epicenters of imminent extinctions.

Butterfly Conservation Initiative
MYBFCI.org
Dedicated to the conservation of threatened, endangered, and vulnerable North American butterflies and the habitats that sustain them.

Butterfly Project
ButterflyProjectNYC.org
A grassroots, volunteer-led, organization of New Yorkers with a common goal—to promote and assist in the planting and preservation of native plants in urban, public spaces in order to create and strengthen resources for native pollinators.

Center for Watershed Protection
Cwp.org
A national organization working to protect watersheds.

Defenders of Wildlife
Endangered.org/tag/defenders-of-wildlife
A national conservation organization promoting biodiversity and protecting wildlife.

Earthwork's No Dirty Gold Campaign
NoDirtyGold.org
An international campaign working to ensure that gold mining operations respect human rights and the environment.

E.hormone
e.hormone.tulane.edu
A central conduit providing accurate, timely information and educational resources at the cutting edge of environmental signaling research. Environmental signaling encompasses the many ways plants and animals use chemical signals to communicate

life-driving information, to respond to physical or biological stimuli, and to talk to each other.

Endangered Species Coalition
Endangered.org
Their mission is to stop the human-caused extinction of our nation's at-risk species.

Environmental Working Group
EWG.org
A national organization working to protect human health by using research and education with a focus on harmful chemicals and products. Their website includes "EWG's Guide to Infant Formula and Baby Bottles."
— *EWG.org/skindeep:* Skin Deep Cosmetics Database is the searchable database of toxic ingredients in cosmetic and personal care products.

International Climate Action Network
ClimateNetwork.org
A global network of non-governmental organizations working on climate change.

National Alliance for Breastfeeding Advocacy
NABA-BreastFeeding.org
Dedicated to the protection, promotion and support of breastfeeding in the US.

National Audubon Society
Aubudon.org
A national organization with many local chapters conserving ecosystems and protecting birds.

National Resources Defense Council
NRDC.org
A national environmental action organization using law and science to protect the planet's wildlife.

Peregrine Fund
PeregrineFund.org
A non-profit organization dedicated to saving birds of prey from extinction.

Polar Bears International
PolarBearsInternational.org
Working globally to save polar bears and their habitats.

Raptor Resource Project

RaptorResource.org

This non-profit specializes in the preservation of falcons, eagles, ospreys, hawks, and owls.

Reconciliation Australia

Reconciliation.org.au

The national expert body on reconciliation in Australia and their vision is to wake to a reconciled, just and equitable Australia.

River Network

River.Network.org

An online hub of state and local organizations protecting waterways.

Safer Chemicals, Healthy Families

SaferChemicals.org

A coalition of more than 450 organizations and 11 million individuals working to reform our outdated toxic chemical laws.

Save the Redwoods League

SavetheRedwoods.org

Their mission is to protect and restore redwood forests and connect people with their peace and beauty so these wonders of the natural world flourish.

Sempervirens Fund

Sempervirens.org

Creates protected parks for old growth redwoods in the Santa Cruz area.

Sierra Club

SierraClub.org

The oldest environmental organization in the United States working on a broad array of environmental initiatives including: climate change, promoting clean energy and environmental justice.

Society for Ecological Restoration

Ser.org

Their purpose is to promote ecological restoration as a means of sustaining the diversity of life on Earth and re-establishing an ecologically healthy relationship between nature and culture.

The Xerces Society

Xerces.org

A global organization striving to conserve invertebrates like butterflies, dragonflies and crabs.

About the Artist

Deborah Kennedy's writing explores themes related to the natural world and ecology. Environmental issues including the decline in bird and butterfly populations, endocrine disruption, and our deep connections to the larger natural world are the focus of her work. Recently, the Bay Area Poets Coalition awarded first prize to her poem, "Fate of My Son."

Deborah Kennedy also works as an artist and has exhibited in California and Europe in numerous solo and group shows featuring objects, conceptually-based installations, and public art also focusing on ecological and social themes. Kennedy is best known for creating the last important artworks on the surface of the Berlin Wall six months before it was demolished. The best know of these works, a civic-specific installation, *Schrift am der Mauer* or *Writing on the Wall*, featured the hopes and fears of ordinary people from East Berlin, West Berlin and America inscribed on metal plates. The inner thoughts and feelings of people from both sides of Berlin and from both sides of the Atlantic communicated together on the Wall, itself once a potent emblem of both hope and fear, East and West.

In 1999, her solo exhibition, *Nature Speaks*, was presented in the de Saisset Museum of Santa Clara University and featured three large-scale installations. She has received many awards including a three-year California Arts Council grant to work with at-risk youth on graffiti murals, and an Artist's Fellowship for Installation Arts from the Arts Council of Santa Clara County, California. Reviews of her work have appeared in numerous publications including: *Artweek*, *The San Jose Mercury News*, and two books published in Germany featured her work.

Kennedy teaches college classes in art and art history and presents at ecology conferences and poetry readings. She and her family celebrate winter holidays in Yosemite where the stars provide more than enough holiday lights. She often hikes in an urban riparian corridor finding osprey, hawks and herons and regularly moongazes — watching for moon bows, earthshine and other modern miracles.